While most of us aren't full-time, vocational evangelists, we're all capable of having God use us to bear witness to Christ's work in our life. In *Good News for a Change*, my friend Matt helps us overcome our fears and grasp the practical ways we all can be liberated to join God's timeless quest to build his Kingdom, life by life.

KEVIN PALAU, president, Luis Palau Association

I don't like books on evangelism. As a general rule, sharing the good news of Jesus is learned better on the street than in the classroom. But this book is different. Very different. For it is crafted by someone who knows the streets and has years of experience sharing Jesus with real, everyday, normal people. This book does two things: It presents the good news of Jesus as both good and news. In an age of fake news, this teaches us how we can share the good news, not fake goods, in a way that is good and life-giving. Mikalatos should get an award for this book. It is a masterpiece.

A. J. SWOBODA, PhD, pastor and author of *Subversive Sabbath: The Surprising Power of Rest in a Nonstop World*

Matt Mikalatos is a brilliant writer and teacher. *Good News for a Change* combines solid Bible teaching, relevant issues, compassion, humor, and practical application. The reader benefits from both the *why?* and *how?* of evangelism as Matt shares actual conversations from personal experience with clear, sharp, thoughtful insights. I appreciate Matt's humble, learner posture and the thorough research used in addressing our current social landscape. Refreshing, pertinent, challenging, relatable—I highly recommend this book!

VIVIAN MABUNI, speaker and author of *Warrior in Pink: A Story of Cancer, Community, and the God Who Comforts*

Every Christian I know is afraid of evangelism. We all know we're supposed to do it, but none of us is any good at it. In *Good News for a Change*, Matt Mikalatos has shared with us his gifts as an evangelist. With the expertise of a teacher, the love of a mentor, and the passion of an artist, Matt demystifies the process of telling people about Jesus. As every great thinker does, he shows us that we don't need more information. We need a new way to look at the work God is already doing in our lives. *Good News for a Change* is a practical, inspiring, and exciting return to our first love—and what's easier to share than that?

JR FORASTEROS, pastor and author of *Empathy for the Devil: Finding Ourselves in the Villains of the Bible*

In today's argument culture, Christians are leery to share their perspective. After all, who wants to get into a heated religious argument with a friend or coworker? Mikalatos reminds us that *everyone* along the social spectrum enjoys hearing one thing—good news. Through engaging stories, helpful communication exercises, and insightful handling of the Scriptures, readers are reminded that the story of Jesus is not only inherently good but also attractive to others.

> **TIM MUEHLHOFF, PhD**, professor of communication studies, Biola University, and author of *Winsome Persuasion: Christian Influence in a Post-Christian World*

A lot of us who grew up in a Christian fundamental environment often felt like we were doing Christianity wrong. If we didn't "win souls" by telling people they were sinners destined for the fiery pits of hell, then we must have been ashamed of Jesus, which meant we probably didn't truly love God. At best, evangelism was an icky sales pitch chore we were required to do. At worst, we may have driven away loved ones and developed resentment or worse toward the God who saves. In *Good News for a Change*, Matt reminds us why the truth of Jesus is such good news. Sharing in that truth is a privilege—exciting and beautiful, and not even a little icky.

> **CLAY MORGAN**, author of *Undead: Revived, Resuscitated, Reborn*

I loved this book! Evangelism can be scary. We often love Jesus but are intimidated to talk about him with others. Fortunately, Matt Mikalatos is here to the rescue: with funny stories from his personal experience and illuminating insights from Scripture, he breaks down stereotypes of stuffy evangelism so you can enter the freedom and joy of fresh, creative, respectful, and down-to-earth ways to catalyze life-giving conversations about Jesus. I plan to use this when training others and have already begun putting some of his ideas into practice myself!

JOSHUA RYAN BUTLER, pastor at Imago Dei Community in Portland, Oregon, and author of *The Skeletons in God's Closet* and *The Pursuing God*

In the past twenty years, there has been a revolution in our understanding of evangelism and what it means to share the good news. Without fanfare or folderol, Matt Mikalatos takes the best of what we've learned and gives us a toolbox of creative resources and handy instruments that can help us lift up Christ in energizing and compelling ways.

LEONARD SWEET, author, professor, and founder and chief contributor to preachthestory.com

GOOD NEWS FOR A CHANGE

GOOD
NEWS
FOR A
CHANGE

MATT MIKALATOS

NAVPRESS

A NavPress resource published in alliance
with Tyndale House Publishers, Inc.

NavPress is the publishing ministry of The Navigators, an international Christian organization and leader in personal spiritual development. NavPress is committed to helping people grow spiritually and enjoy lives of meaning and hope through personal and group resources that are biblically rooted, culturally relevant, and highly practical.

For more information, visit www.NavPress.com.

Good News for a Change: How to Talk to Anyone about Jesus

Copyright © 2018 by Matt Mikalatos. All rights reserved.

A NavPress resource published in alliance with Tyndale House Publishers, Inc.

NAVPRESS and the NAVPRESS logo are registered trademarks of NavPress, The Navigators, Colorado Springs, CO. *TYNDALE* is a registered trademark of Tyndale House Publishers, Inc. Absence of ® in connection with marks of NavPress or other parties does not indicate an absence of registration of those marks.

The Team:
Don Pape, Publisher
Caitlyn Carlson, Acquisitions Editor
Elizabeth Symm, Copy Editor
Eva Winters, Designer

Cover photograph of chicken costume copyright © Eric Chuang/Getty Images. All rights reserved.

Back cover photograph of grunge paper copyright © PhotoAlto/James Hardy/Getty Images. All rights reserved.

The author is represented by Ambassador Literary Agency, Nashville, TN.

Some of the anecdotal illustrations in this book are true to life and are included with the permission of the persons involved. All other illustrations are composites of real situations, and any resemblance to people living or dead is purely coincidental.

For information about special discounts for bulk purchases, please contact Tyndale House Publishers at csresponse@tyndale.com, or call 1-800-323-9400.

Cataloging-in-Publication Data is available.

ISBN 978-1-63146-856-8

Printed in the United States of America

24   23   22   21   20   19   18
7   6   5   4   3   2   1

TO MY SZ FAMILY, who lived this book.

You continue to inspire me, and I love each one of you.

CONTENTS

INTRODUCTION

Good News about Evangelism

MY FRIEND RICK came to Christ while watching a cigar-smoking '80s televangelist who wore sunglasses and strange hats and made long, rambling speeches punctuated by sudden cut-aways to a band playing Jesus songs. Years later, Rick, now a pastor, visited the televangelist's church, excited to see the man who had led him to Christ. He left disappointed by the nonsensical sermon and uncertain whether the televangelist knew Jesus himself.

I know a woman who came to Christ after two cult missionaries visited her house and she misunderstood their message. Despite their intentions, she prayed to receive Christ and started attending a local evangelical church.

I know a man who came to Christ while smoking pot with a buddy. His friend started crying and saying what a terrible Christian he was, that he used pot and misused alcohol and wished he could get his life together. My friend was interested in the whole concept, met Jesus, stopped smoking pot, and joined staff with a Christian nonprofit.

I've met people who came to Christ after getting picked up by believers while hitchhiking. I've talked with more than one person who came to Christ through Billy Graham's ministry. I know people who came to Christ through street preachers, vacation Bible schools, televangelists, neighbors, family members, miraculous healings, sermons at funerals, sermons at weddings, and conversations at Christmas parties. I know of one person who came to him through an inter-action with a Christian homeless woman. And once I met a guy who came to Christ out of Hinduism because while bowing down to a (literal) sacred cow, it kicked him in the head. "I knew there had to be a better way," he said.

I especially love my friend John's story. In college, he joined a Christian student group and went with them on a weeklong mission trip to Las Vegas, where they were going to "evangelize" the tourists. Part of the training was learning to use the *Four Spiritual Laws*, a religious tract for sharing the gospel. Before going out to share it with others, John read the booklet himself. After reading the basics of the good news and a "salvation prayer," he encountered a key question: "Does this prayer express the desire of your heart?" John decided it did and *led himself to Christ*. That's a good start to a mission trip.

God brings people to himself however he pleases. The good news really is good news, and it breaks through the noise around us in countless ways.

It's tempting to think, then, that we have no role to play. God could, after all, train parrots to share the good news and send them out into the world to perch in trees and say, "Jesus loves you" and "You're a sinner" and so on. Then we would never have to feel weird by talking to someone about Jesus; we could just make sure to put some crackers near the homes of our friends who don't know God and trust his feathered evangelists to make things clear.

But—and this is important—just because God can use any means to bring someone to himself doesn't mean he doesn't want us involved. While God can use any means, any person, any situation to speak good news into someone's life, he offers us the privilege and blessing of partnering together to do that. It's a gift to get to share good news, to participate in God's work in someone else's life.

I love my friend John, and I'm so pleased he led himself to Christ . . . and I wish I could have been a more central part of that process! To be in that conversation with John would have let me see firsthand how God was at work in John's life, would have given me new insights into what exactly this good news means. That's a big deal, to participate with God in communicating the good news. And we seem to forget that, or we're so intimidated by the idea of this thing we call evangelism that we don't try. After all, for a lot of us, our first response to someone coming to Christ isn't wishing we could have been involved. It's not hard to imagine sitting down with a neighbor who has just come to Jesus and thinking, with some relief, *Whew! I guess I don't have to share the gospel with them after all!*

And I get it. I do. Over the years, we've turned evangelism into a transactional thing, where all the pressure is on us to make the sale. In our consumer culture, we think we have to convince someone they really need this salvation thing, and we're a failure if they don't get it.

It's scary. It's uncomfortable. It's awkward. And it also doesn't have to be that way. It *shouldn't* be that way.

I worked for a less-than-reputable photography studio for a while during college. My job was to man the telephone in a little back room and dial through a list of numbers. When the person on the other end picked up, I started into a whole script: "Good news! My less-than-reputable photography studio is running a sale on portraits!" (Okay, maybe not quite that, but close.) I had a script for what to say to their objections (Them: "I'm too ugly for pictures." Me: "Sir, no one is ugly to their loved ones.") and to their questions about pets ("Legal pets are allowed."), taking photos naked ("Um . . . no."), and how they could convince their grandchildren to send pictures more often ("Portraits make a wonderful gift."). All the while, my manager stood nearby, arms folded as we made cold calls, shaking his head when we answered the questions wrong and marking our referrals and sales next to our names on a whiteboard.

When it comes to evangelism, some of us, or maybe a lot of us, picture God a lot like that manager: the disapproving, scowling overseer who watches from a distance, disappointed that we're not working harder, selling better, dialing more. And that terrible misunderstanding of evangelism—the forced sales pitch—comes from a fundamental misunderstanding of the good news.

At the photo studio, we needed rhetorical tricks and scripts and sales techniques because our product was terrible and was always on sale. The supposed good news was false. (You may have gathered that I didn't last long there.)

With the gospel, we need to get past the sales tactics and high-pressure techniques *because we don't need them.* A well-honed sales pitch reveals that we've forgotten the gospel is, at its core, good news. It was good news for us, and it's good news for the people with whom we're sharing.

I hated my job selling those portraits, and if you think of evangelism this way, it makes sense to hate it, too. But that's not what evangelism is.

Evangelism is, first and foremost, *us participating with the Holy Spirit to tell people about God and his love for them* and to invite them into a relationship with him. Because we're doing the work together with the Holy Spirit, we can trust that God will pick up the slack where we're failing. God wants us to participate, but it is God who ultimately makes the good news clear to our listeners. In fact, Paul said that even when someone shared the good news with evil motives, he was still happy the message was going out.[1]

That's the good news about evangelism: If you're doing it at all, you're doing it right. There are people who will line up to tell you the "right way" to talk about Jesus or say you're not truly sharing the gospel unless you do it a specific way, but if you're doing it at all, that's something God can and will use. It's difficult to do evangelism the wrong way.

That's why the book you are about to read is not about

judgment. It's not designed to make you feel guilty about evangelism or to make you feel bad for the way you do it. Nobody's going to pull out a scorecard or a whiteboard with your name on it to keep track of your "sales." The point of this book is to talk about ways we can more fully participate with God in the beautiful work of bringing human beings back into the loving embrace of the one who made them.

We'll talk about the gospel and what it is, how it functions, and what it means to be witnesses. We'll consider whether the gospel "changes" for different people or is one precise message for everyone. We'll discuss how to talk about Jesus with coworkers, your family, and those in your neighborhood—without looking like a crazy person.

Mainly, we're going to talk about how to have conversations about Jesus where even people hostile to Christianity thank you afterward and feel loved and excited about the conversation—and where you feel excited and comfortable with the conversation too. That sounds crazy, I know, but it's true. We'll discuss some tools that will give you confidence to talk to anyone you know, anyone you meet, about the excellent good news of Jesus.

Each chapter will have questions to consider, exercises to try, and suggestions for joining God in the beautiful plan of redemption. I pray you will find these resources helpful, energizing, and transformative.

Using the underpinning philosophy in this book, I've led an atheist Bible study; shared the good news with a millionaire on an airplane while she clutched my hand and prayed we wouldn't crash; sat beneath an oak tree with a Satanist, chatting about the beauty of Jesus; and seen a Buddhist accept Christ after a fifteen-minute conversation.

If you think those are things you can't possibly do, just wait. I promise, this really is the good news about evangelism: It's much easier than you thought. Talking to people about the good news is one of the most fun, interesting, and exciting adventures you could possibly embark on. You are going to enjoy it! And along the way, God is going to change some lives.

That's the best news of all.

CHAPTER 1

THE GOSPEL ACCORDING TO GOD

The Unchanging Message of the Good News

THERE WAS A KNOCK at my dorm-room door.

I opened it to find another student standing there, a young man I didn't know. Before I could say a word, he said, "You need to stop smoking pot, stop sleeping with your girlfriend, and come to Jesus."

Startled and unsure what was happening, I said, "My girlfriend lives eight hours away, and I've never smoked pot."

He shook his head, as if I had completely misunderstood his message, and said again, "You need to stop smoking pot, stop sleeping with your girlfriend, and come to Jesus."

"Listen," I said. "I don't smoke, and I couldn't sleep with

my girlfriend if I wanted to. She lives on the other side of the state."

"I know you love pot," he said. "I know you sleep around. But you've got to come to Jesus."

"I'm already a Christian," I said.

He threw his arms wide, a huge grin on his face, and shouted, "Brother!"

That was not an enjoyable way to hear the so-called good news. Could the Holy Spirit use that young man's passionate initiative to bring someone to saving knowledge of him? Absolutely. Would I like to go back in time and give that kid some gentle advice? Yes, please.

Sometimes we forget the gospel is good news. We think we have to battle people with the gospel, that we have to confront them and beat them down. There's a reason the term "Bible thumper" exists. We think we're in a war and we have to "win people to Christ." It's a contest, a battle, a game, a conflict.

In that context, it's not "good news." It's propaganda. And when we see evangelism as conflict, we immediately put our listeners on the defensive. When I was a college student, "stop smoking pot, stop sleeping with your girlfriend, and come to Jesus" was unrecognizable to me as good news. My would-be evangelist told me, "You need a different moral code." That's not good news; that's a philosophical argument waiting to happen.

So if the good news isn't "stop sinning and come to Jesus," what is it?

Let's Talk about Jesus

The gospel is ultimately about Jesus.

There is an awful lot of good news about Jesus, and it's not just that he died for our sins and was raised again on the third day. Healing the sick, that was good news. Being born to Mary, that was good news. The forgiveness he gave to those caught up in evil behavior in their lives, that's good news. The way he interacted with women as people worthy of respect, that's good news. His ascension, the Transfiguration, the time he stayed in the Temple when his parents were walking home and he was "lost" from them for a few days: good news. His parables, his teachings, the feeding of the gigantic crowds—these things are all good news.

Any "gospel presentation" is, by definition, only shorthand for the "full gospel." There's no such thing as a complete gospel presentation, because Jesus is an eternal person, and all the news about him is good; which means part of the work of eternity will be getting to know him and growing in our knowledge of the good news. We don't know the entire gospel now, nor will we ever, because we will never exhaust the knowledge of Jesus' goodness. The good news we know is amazing, and the good news as we get to know Jesus only deepens and grows.

Nevertheless, there is a sort of "core" gospel that we'll refer to as the "universal gospel." It's the good news that is true for every person on earth, no matter their background, culture, ethnicity, or social status. It's good news that may take some work to understand for some, but most of us, when we think of evangelism, think precisely of this universal gospel: How do I tell someone the core, salvific truth of the good news?

My favorite place to start the universal good news is with the most famous Bible verse of them all, John 3:16: "God so loved the world that he gave his one and only Son, that whoever believes in him shall not perish but have eternal life." The most basic, core message of the gospel is "believe in Jesus and receive eternal life."

This one verse also tells us God's *motivation* in saving humanity: He loves us. That's part of the gospel, too, and for many of us, the most unbelievable, baffling bit. I've had more than one person tell me it's the one thing about the gospel that they just cannot believe.

People start throwing up all sorts of objections to this simple idea, like "You don't know what I've done. God couldn't possibly love someone like me."

But as Paul writes in Romans 5:8, *While we were still sinners, Christ died for us* (NKJV). Christ died for sinners. Why? What was his motivation? Because *God loved the world so much*. Jesus didn't come into the world to condemn the world but to save it. If we love him, it's because he loved us first.[1]

The simplest, core bit of the universal gospel is all in John 3:16. It doesn't spell everything out—it implies the other pieces, assuming maybe you already know them. For instance, it doesn't say "All have sinned and fall short of the glory of God"[2] or "The wages of sin is death"[3] (both part of the universal gospel in the sense they are the bad news that the good news answers), but it says that if we believe in Jesus, we don't have to perish. It sort of assumes we know that everyone dies rather than spelling it all out for us.

I have plenty of friends who, if they were going to choose a passage to boil the gospel down to its core bit, would rather use 1 Corinthians 15:1-6:

> Now, brothers and sisters, I want to remind you of the gospel I preached to you, which you received and on which you have taken your stand. By this gospel you are saved, if you hold firmly to the word I preached to you. Otherwise, you have believed in vain.
>
> For what I received I passed on to you as of first importance: that Christ died for our sins according to the Scriptures, that he was buried, that he was raised on the third day according to the Scriptures, and that he appeared to Cephas, and then to the Twelve. After that, he appeared to more than five hundred of the brothers and sisters at the same time, most of whom are still living, though some have fallen asleep.

This passage answers a question we might have had after reading John 3:16: What exactly do I have to believe about Jesus to be saved? Paul (the author of 1 Corinthians) lays it out for us: Christ (the Savior sent from God) died for our sins and also came back from the dead to show God's power over death. Our sins, Jesus' death, and Jesus' resurrection come together as the seed of the gospel. It's still a sort of shorthand—it's not the whole gospel, but it's a piece that lodges like a seed into the soil of the human heart.

Maybe that's what the young man at my dorm-room door was trying to get at: "Stop sinning and come to Jesus." But somehow his words didn't communicate that universal gospel to me. What I heard was, "Agree with my morality and convert to my religion." I didn't recognize the good news in what he said . . . or at least in the way he said it.

At nearly the same time I was talking to that young man in Southern California, Krista, the woman whom I would one day marry, was on a tour in southern China with her college history class.

Krista asked her tour guide, "What god do you worship?" She was from an ethnic minority in those southern regions.

"I worship the god of my tribe," the young woman replied. "What god do you worship?"

Krista said, "I worship a God of the whole world . . . a God for every tribe on earth."

Shocked, the tour guide said, "I have never heard of a god for all people! Tell me more."

There's that good news again . . . a God for the whole world. God loved the whole world, which includes you and me, Krista, and a tour guide from southern China. So the thing about the universal gospel isn't that it's not attractive, or hopeful, or life changing. It's all those things and more. But sometimes we forget how individually, personally life changing it really is. We are so worried about getting the "facts" right that we forget to check if the person we're talking to even gets why it's good news. But once we understand the kaleidoscopic beauty of the universal gospel—for ourselves and for every person around us—everything changes.

Reflection Questions

1. Restate what the young man said at my dorm-room door to make it sound more like good news. Is there a way to keep his basic message but say it in a way that reveals good news? How much would you need to know about the person listening to your message to make the good news clear?

2. What does God's motivation in sending Jesus suggest about our own motivation in sharing Christ? What should we do if we find ourselves motivated by fear, guilt, judgment, or shame instead of love?

3. Read the 1 Corinthians 15 passage again and think back to the time before you knew Jesus. If someone had come to you and read that passage, alone and without explanation, how would you have responded? Would you have recognized it as good news or not?

Exercises

1. Get together with a Christian friend and take turns sharing the good news with one another, using only Scripture as your springboard to conversation. The first person gets to use any verse they like from John 3. The next person can use 1 Corinthians 15:1-6. Then look together at the "Romans Road": Romans 3:23; 6:23; 5:8; 10:9; and 5:1. (This will be easiest if you stick to the order I listed them in.) This is a no-risk way to practice good news conversations . . . and it will help you keep the ideas of the universal good news in mind.

2. Choose a verse or verses from the Bible that really speak to you about good news, and memorize them. Memorization is a great way to get the good news to seep into our bones so it becomes second nature. If you have a hard time memorizing, just text the verse to yourself twice a day, once in the morning and once at night, until you don't need to look at your Bible anymore. (Obviously, don't just forward the text, you cheater—type it in each time.) Don't worry too much about getting it all word-for-word—the concepts are just as important as the precise wording.

CHAPTER 2

THE GOSPEL ACCORDING TO YOU

The Personal Message of the Good News

"WHAT IS THE GOSPEL?"

I was at an evangelism training with a group of millennial professionals in Portland, Oregon, and I was curious to see how these people would answer this all-important question. After all, like we just discussed in the last chapter, it's hard to talk about the gospel unless you really understand the gospel, right?

The answers we wrote on the wall will sound familiar. They said things like

- God came to earth for our sins.
- The life, death, and resurrection of Jesus.
- The story of Jesus.

9

· We can be saved and go to heaven.

Many of us, when we're asked, "What is the gospel?" will default to answers like these and stop there. They're great answers that come largely from that 1 Corinthians 15 passage, where Paul talks about "the gospel [he] preached," which was "Christ died for our sins according to the Scriptures," "he was buried," and "he was raised on the third day according to the Scriptures." It's the "universal gospel" we talked about in the last chapter. So far so good.

But we shouldn't stop there. Next I asked them, "What is *good news* about Jesus?"

We started another column to the right of the first. They said things like

· He is wise.
· He cares for me.
· He is a relatable person.
· We have a good relationship.
· He comforts me when I am hurting.

That certainly sounds like good news, to be in relationship with a person like that! What's fascinating, of course, is that when I asked them "What does the word *gospel* mean?" they immediately said, "Good news."

"But why were your answers so different for those two questions, then?"

They weren't sure. But somehow *gospel* meant broad

theological statements and *good news* meant personal things. Part of it is that the word *gospel* has become religious jargon. It's a word you'll mostly hear used in a theological context, like at church (unless you like Gospel music; or if you live in the southern United States, you might hear that something is "the Gospel truth"). But overall, it's a word used primarily in religious circles, and because of that, the word evokes theological answers. The "gospel" is theological constructs, but "good news" is personal.

This was a crowd of West Coast millennials, and maybe your answers about good news would be different. But that's an important point: What is most meaningful about the good news of Jesus for someone else might be different than what's most compelling about the good news to you or me. The Gospel according to Me might be expressed differently than the Gospel according to You.

What Is Your Good News?

The idea of a gospel that is both unchanging and deeply personal, both the same for everyone and completely different for each of us, sounds perplexing, but it's a solid theological concept.

The Greek word *euangelion* (εὐαγγέλιον) translates exactly to the words *good news* or *good message*. The term was originally used in wartime. When a distant battle took place, runners would bring messages back to the city, letting residents know what was happening on the front line.

Those who brought good news from the war were called *evangelists*—"those who bring good news": The good news that your city's army was beating the enemy. The good news that your father, your uncle, your brother had survived.

Over time, the word leaked into the secular world, and the Greeks would talk about the *evangel* of everyday experience: The good news that Dad got a raise. The good news that Mom's health scare was just that, a scare. The good news that your neighbor had a new grandchild.

When the Bible writers referred to "the *evangel* of Jesus" (or as it might appear in our English translations, "the *gospel of Jesus*"), anyone reading would have absolutely understood the word to mean "the *good news* of Jesus."

Just to be clear, the English word *gospel* itself doesn't appear in Scripture. It's a Middle English word (as I like to tell my kids, "Middle English is, you know, what the hobbits spoke") and first appeared as *godspel*—*god*, meaning "good," and *spel*, meaning "story." To pronounce it correctly, just pretend you are Sean Connery and maybe put a few marbles in your mouth: "*Gaawdshpiel.*"

Gospel in its original, Middle English meaning was a great translation of *euangelion* because it meant something very close to "good news." Over time, "gospel" slowly became a church-only word, but the fact remains that what the original Greek meant, what the Middle English word meant, and what the modern word *should* mean is this: good news.

I don't get nervous telling people good news. I get excited.

I might get nervous about "the gospel," but not about good news.

We realize, of course, that Matthew, Mark, Luke, and John each wrote a "Gospel." Each writer's "good news" about Jesus and the coming Kingdom was slightly different from the others' good news. There was enormous overlap in their good news, but there are some things, for instance, that John thought needed to be emphasized that no one else mentioned, and vice versa. There were things Matthew saw that Luke doesn't mention. Mark related experiences that John didn't think were worth including.

In 2 Timothy 2:8-9, Paul says his good news is "Jesus Christ, raised from the dead, *descended from David*."[4] I've never once shared Jesus' ancestry as my own good news, but for Paul it was an essential part of the gospel. For Matthew, too! In fact, he starts his Gospel with that very thing. I wouldn't suggest starting a conversation with "Hey, do you know who Jesus' great-great-great-great-grandpa was?" but I wouldn't be mad if you wanted to try it, either.

Even Jesus (or maybe I should say especially Jesus) had a unique take on the good news. Matthew 4:23 says that Jesus went from town to town preaching the good news—and then in chapters 5–7, Matthew shares Jesus' gospel presentation: the Sermon on the Mount. Imagine a gospel presentation from Jesus himself!

Here's where I'm going with all this: Each of us, as a follower of Jesus, has good news to share. There will, of course, be a lot of overlap in our stories because of the universal gospel. We all believe Jesus died for our sins and rose from the dead. We all believe Jesus is God, sent to earth as a human because of God's love for humanity.

But we also each have our own good news—intensely personal good news that has come about because of our relationship with Jesus and how he has interacted with us, our families, and our communities. We have good news that comes from our own history with God.

Right now, I am going through a difficult time where one of my best friends is struggling with terminal cancer. It's immensely painful for me, for her family, for my family, and for her many friends. I know that doesn't sound like good news. But there have been these intense moments of peace— not months at a time, not even weeks at a time—just these moments where I feel God's presence and I know my friend is going to be safe and well in God's presence, whether that's here with us (our preference) or in his heavenly Kingdom. So for me, today, this moment as I am typing, part of my good news is simply the presence of God that brings peace in the midst of deep pain, suffering, and grief. That's just me sharing my experience: what I have seen and heard from God in the last few months.

Scripture has a word for this. Jesus said we are his *witnesses*[5]—and not that we will be or should be or ought to be his witnesses. No, we *are* his witnesses. The Greek word for witness is *martus* (μάρτυς). It was a legal term used in Greek courts. If we were to try to choose the perfect word to translate *martus* into English, we couldn't choose a better word than *witness*.

Now, the word *witness* can be terrifying to us. We worry people will reject us . . . or that we don't have the right words to say . . . or that people might be offended or think we're saying they're wrong and we're right. We worry the person we're talking to might know more than us.

Once when I preached at a church and said we would be talking about witnessing, people stood to leave. I called after them, "Hey! Come back! It's okay—there's no need to be afraid!" And that's absolutely true. To do their jobs, witnesses only have to be honest about what they have experienced. That's it. They don't have to be experts. They don't have to understand the law. They don't need to study for years. Good witnesses do one thing: share the truth about what they have seen.

We see this often in Scripture, but my favorite description is in 1 John 1:1-3, where John says,

That which was from the beginning, which we have heard, which we have seen with our eyes, which we have looked at and our hands have touched—this we proclaim concerning the Word of life. The life appeared; we have seen it and testify to it, and we proclaim to you the eternal life, which was with the Father and has appeared to us. We proclaim to you what we have seen and heard, so that you also may have fellowship with us. And our fellowship is with the Father and with his Son, Jesus Christ.

To be a witness is not a complicated thing. It doesn't require seminary degrees and reading Bible studies or books about evangelism (including this one!). It only requires that you share what you have seen and heard and experienced with Jesus. If we're terrified of it, it's only because we've forgotten that our job isn't to convince people—it's to tell them, in a way they can understand, what we have seen and heard and experienced.

So, what have *you* seen? What have you heard? What have you looked at, and what have your hands touched? Where has God showed up when you didn't have hope any longer? When has he surprised you? What did God do in your life this year . . . this month . . . this week? How has Christ changed you, your relationships, or your world for the better? What is your good news about Jesus, and are you ready to share it with others?

Reflection Questions

1. Do you personally feel a difference between the words *gospel* and *good news*? If I asked you to make two lists, one titled "Good News about Jesus" and the other "The Gospel," would those lists be identical or different? If different, how so? If the same and the terms are interchangeable, which do you prefer? Why?

2. If an acquaintance asked you, "What is the good news about Jesus?" or "What is the gospel?" how would you answer?

3. How did you come to know Jesus? Who told you about him? What was the process like? Were there terms that confused you, or did you understand immediately?

4. Read Matthew 5–7, the "Sermon on the Mount," keeping in mind this is a presentation of the good news about the Kingdom. What observations do you make? How is it a gospel presentation? Why are Jesus' words here good news?

Exercises

1. What is your good news? Make a list of your personal "good news" about Jesus. This can include theological, universal good news (like "Jesus died for me") but should also include personal good news (like "God comforted me when I lost a loved one" or "The weather was beautiful today" or any number of other things, big or small).

2. Choose to share some of your good news with someone this week. Don't worry about "sharing the gospel" for now. Just tell someone something good about having Jesus in your life.

CHAPTER 3

THE GOSPEL ACCORDING TO "THEM"

Everyone Wants Good News

"WHY ARE CHRISTIAN SONGS SO CREEPY?"

I was teaching at a conference called Big Break. It took place in Panama City Beach, Florida, which is a mecca for partying college students over spring break. Cru (formerly called Campus Crusade for Christ) held a conference every year where about a thousand Christian kids would come together each week—not to drink and party, but to sing praise songs, receive training in evangelism, and hit the beaches to talk to people about Jesus.

Not everyone at this evangelism conference was a Christian. Every year, for one reason or another, a handful of nonbelieving students showed up. You can imagine it might be a little weird. One particular student (let's call him Brandon) had been dragged along by his sister, who had just decided to follow Jesus the month before. She wanted her brother to come hang out with her and her new Christian friends for the week.

One night after I had spoken, I invited non-Christians to come hang out with me and discuss "How to survive a Christian conference when you're not a Christian" as well as the basic beliefs of Christianity (this, actually, was a brief presentation of the "universal gospel"). Brandon, along with five other students, decided to come. During our conversation, he asked me, "Why are Christian songs so creepy?"

"Can you give me an example?"

"Yeah, that one song was so weird: 'Consume me from the inside out'?! What, you want God to eat your guts? It's so gross."

I didn't laugh, but I did grin at him. I was so delighted by the question. The lyrics are from the song "From the Inside Out," by an Australian praise group called Hillsong Worship, and it's sung often and with great gusto by Christians all over the world. I'm guessing there weren't many people sitting in church and thinking to themselves, *What am I saying? Do I really want God to devour my innards?*

"Anything else?" I asked him.

"Yeah. Why do Christians hate sheep? You're always singing about slaying them, about taking baths in their blood. It's weird and it's gross. I don't understand."

Believe it or not, Brandon's creeped-out feelings about

Christian praise music were the key to him hearing the good news about Jesus—but not the good news I expected. And I'm pretty sure it's not the good news you are expecting, either.

I started by telling him it was perfectly normal to think those things were weird. Then, using simple words and leaving out the more complicated details, I explained to him about the sheep. I told him a short version of the Passover story. I told him about the Jewish sacrificial system and how sheep were killed as an atonement for the wrongdoings of the people.

"That's horrible," Brandon said. "Do they still do that?"

"No. Let me explain that, too."

After that, he was still interested and asking questions, so I went on. Then I got to the important part—the good news!

"So," I said, "people deserve to die because of the wrong things they've done. But Jesus—God—came to earth as a human being, and even though he had done nothing wrong, he was killed. He came back to life to show God's power over death and to invite us into relationship with him! Because of Jesus, people don't have to die. They can choose to live forever with God."

Mission accomplished. Good news delivered!

"What about the sheep?" Brandon asked.

"What?" I didn't understand. Brandon was off script.

"What about the sheep? Do they still have to die?"

"No," I said. "No, since Jesus died, the sheep don't have to die."

"Wow!" he said, and his face lit up. "That's really good news!"

Brandon's Good News

Jesus didn't die for sheep, did he?

Doing away with slaughtering sheep might be good news for Brandon, but is it really "the gospel"? Can Brandon's relief that sheep don't have to be sacrificed and Christians don't bathe in their blood be sufficient to bring him into a saving relationship with Jesus?

Seeing the good news through the eyes of someone who doesn't yet know Jesus gives me deeper, more beautiful insights into the good news myself. See, the alteration to the sacrificial system has never been part of my personal good news. Maybe it's because I've never had to buy a sheep and walk it up to the Temple. I've never raised an animal only to kill it.

And while Brandon's good news is not part of the *universal* good news, he showed me a truth about the good news of Jesus I hadn't ever really considered: Jesus' death created a fundamental shift in Christian (Jewish at the time) religious practice that allowed us to move away from animal sacrifice. Sheep don't have to be sacrificed anymore, thanks to Jesus.

Brandon's good and beautiful insight has so many interesting theological echoes as I consider the intense care God shows toward all the things he has made and the role humanity is meant to take in caring for animals and creation.

It's beautiful that Brandon's good news became mine, just as mine became his. I learned more about Jesus by seeing him through Brandon's eyes. A nonbeliever shared the good news with *me*! And he gave me the gift of understanding how God was bringing the good news to him, outside of my preset expectations. A lot can happen when we set aside our plans and join God in his endlessly creative pursuit of the ones he loves.

Finding Good News

In the 1960s, Dr. Bill Bright (Cru's/Campus Crusade for Christ's founder) came up with a great way to present the good news in a booklet called the *Four Spiritual Laws*. At the time, most evangelistic conversations started with some version of "You are a sinner"—in other words, "You are terrible and you are going to burn in hell." The good news (of course!) was that Jesus could save you from your fate.

Dr. Bright added a new, simple point before "You are a sinner": "God loves you and has a wonderful plan for your life." This addition wasn't without controversy, which seems strange all these years later. But there were people who felt that starting with God's love "softened the gospel" and would result in a weak, flabby Christianity (online you can find plenty of people talking about how the *Four Spiritual Laws* is unbiblical, which is ludicrous—it's chock full of biblical backup and says only things that have been orthodox theology for centuries).

Notice what Dr. Bright's good news focuses on: forgiveness of sins and eternal life in heaven through Christ. The main message is this: You can live in heaven with God. Or, as the more updated version says, you can know God person-ally. Thousands and thousands of people have decided to fol-low Jesus as a result of this little booklet. I've been there. I've seen it. I know people who came to Christ years ago through its message, and they are still in deep, vibrant relationship with God today.

But let's think about this: The *Four Spiritual Laws*, as great as it is, tends to focus on one selective piece of the good news. What if the person reading it doesn't see anything in there that sounds like good news? What if *heaven* isn't good news to someone?

I've been doing evangelism among college students for the last twenty years or so, and here's what I've noticed: The millennials who started college from the early 2000s through today are increasingly unconcerned about heaven and hell. By unconcerned, I mean precisely that: The issue doesn't mean much to them either way. It's not of inter-est. That's not to say no one cares about it or there aren't individuals who would like to talk about it at length. But overall, as a generation, they don't much care—especially compared to previous generations.

In fact, more than once, I've had a student say something along these lines: "I don't care about what Jesus will do some-day in the future, after I die. What is he going to do today?"

Is eternity in heaven good news? For some people, abso-lutely. But these students shrug when I ask them, replying "I guess so."

You know what really interests these same people? The

idea that God has something to say about our world today: sex trafficking, child abuse, racial discrimination, or the rights of various minority groups. For some people, the statement "God has a plan to fix the broken places in the world" is far better news than "You can go to heaven."

Likewise, many students I talk to today are interested in God's plan for dealing with sin, not because they want to be saved from the "wages of sin"[1] but because they want a way out from the terrible weight of brokenness in their daily lives. They'd much rather hear how Christ can help them become better people today than hear about how Christ can save them from sin-related spiritual death in the future.

The Bible is clear that both these things are true: Jesus can save us from the penalty of sin as well as the daily side effects of sin (the theologians call the first one justification and the second sanctification). If sanctification is more interesting than justification to someone, why wouldn't I steer the conversation to the more relevant topic? Both are good news. But which one is better news to the person I'm talking to?

And by the way, that's precisely what Dr. Bright did in the 1960s. He noticed that starting with "You are a sinner headed to hell" didn't seem like good news to people. So he added some more good news about Jesus. And the news that God loves them and has a wonderful plan for their lives still sounds pretty good to a lot of people.

The Boring Christ

I have a friend, a young woman we'll call Chelsea, who is an atheist. One day she said to me, "You Christians seem to think Jesus is boring." I was shocked. After all, she and I had discussed him at length.

"What do you mean?"

"I mean, you find all these weird ways to bring him up, like you're looking for an angle—a way to make him interesting."

"Can you give me an example?"

"Yeah: like when you do an outreach about porn." (She was a college student. A local Christian club had recently done a "porn survey" among the students and hosted a big night where they were invited to come and talk publicly about pornography. An expert speaker was brought in to share about his own journey into the sex industry's dark corners, and afterward he shared his conversion story.)

"I thought you liked that meeting."

"Oh, yeah. It was interesting. I have a lot of thoughts about the sex industry and pornography. That's how you hooked me. Then, when I was interested, you shoehorned Jesus in there."

"What are you saying?"

Chelsea thought about it for a moment. "I'm saying *you* think sex is more interesting than Jesus."

She wasn't wrong.

We think there is one correct way to share the good news,

and because we need to start in the same place every time ("Jesus died on the cross for your sins and rose on the third day"), we're always trying to find a way to get to that story. The problem is not everyone is interested in that story at first. Not everyone understands how or why it's good news. So instead of finding *their* good news about Jesus, the thing that will draw them along through the story, we find something else they are interested in and tack our good news onto it once we have a captive audience.

This takes many different forms. We have conferences to fix your marriage (answer revealed at the end: Jesus). We invite kids to come play Earth Ball at youth group (followed by a talk about Jesus). We'll do "prophecy seminars" to help people understand what is coming next in this crazy world (Jesus, that's who is coming next!).

Those things aren't wrong, and like I said earlier, they work. Many have come to Christ in these ways, and we shouldn't look down on them.

Nevertheless, Chelsea is right. In journalism, this is called "burying the lede." That's when a reporter writes an article and starts out by talking about things of secondary importance. The news should lead with the most important fact and give you the supplemental information afterward.

Sometimes we bury the lede with Jesus. We don't start with the most important, most interesting news for our audience. It can be a subtle difference, because for some people the good news about Jesus will intersect with other things.

But the "lede" in the good news will always be Jesus, not something else.

The truth is, Jesus is the most fascinating person in the entire universe, and he intersects with everything that interests us in the world. But remember: *The cross is not the only good news about Jesus.* It's really, really good news, but it's not the *only* good news. The incarnate Jesus walked among us for a few decades, and there are millennia's worth of other actions by Jesus, who is God(!), that are also good news. Sometimes, insisting that we *begin* at the cross prevents us from getting to it at all with people. Sometimes, starting with some other piece of good news about Jesus can eventually bring us to the cross too.

And there is a lot of good news to choose from. Jesus, the radical Savior, actually has a plan not just to save your soul but also to repair the broken places in the world. He intends to do away with racism, and sexism, and corrupt prison systems, and flawed governments, and judgmental religious systems, and on and on. If there's a system or a corporation or a person who has harmed you, Jesus has a plan to right that.

We can't limit the good news of Jesus just to the Gospels alone, because the whole of Scripture—and how God intersects with all of life—is the good news of Jesus, because Jesus, after all, is God. Jesus is the God who created the world, who formed quasars and quarks and leptons just by speaking, who designed our brains and emotions and our longing for relationships, and who gave us not just breath and life but also *one another*. The good news weaves its way throughout Scripture, the tapestry of our lives and relationships, and this world God has made.

Everyone on earth, whether they recognize it or not, whether they know it or not, wants to know more about God. They are desperately waiting for someone to start a conversation with them about good news. They're receptive to good news . . . because who isn't? We have this internalized message—the good news about Jesus—that we're ready to communicate, and they're longing to hear it! If we could just find a way to start the conversation, they would be fascinated by Jesus.

Which brings us back to Chelsea. It took me a few times hanging out with her to find what was good news about Jesus for her. It surprised me a little because it was something more traditional and more common than I would have expected. But I finally got a clue about how to transmit the good news message to her in a way I thought she might be able to receive and understand.

"Chelsea," I said, "I'm sorry we've acted like Jesus is less interesting than so many other things in life. Let me make it up to you . . . let me teach you one theology lesson—just one, and then I'll drop it."

"Go ahead."

"Chelsea, Jesus loves you." Such a simple, childlike theology . . . so basic . . . but it's not boring, not at all.

"How could he love me? I'm an atheist. I'm—"

"God knows who you are, what you've done, and what

you believe. And I'm telling you . . . you don't have to believe in Jesus for him to love you."

Chelsea said, "What Jesus is this? I've never heard of a Jesus like this."

"What do you think about that?"

And Chelsea said what all our friends and loved ones will say, what every person on earth will say, if we just give them a chance to enter the conversation. She leaned toward me, eyes wide, and said, "*Tell me more.*"

Reflection Questions

1. Do you believe everyone on earth wants good news? Why or why not?

2. "Jesus is the most fascinating person in the entire universe, and he intersects with everything that interests us in the world." Do you think that's true? Think of all the things that most interest you: Do those things intersect somehow with Jesus in your life?

3. If every person on earth wants to know good news about Jesus, how does that change the way you feel about starting a conversation with people about God?

Exercises

1. Make a list of people who you think are not interested in the good news about Jesus. Who would be hardest to share Christ with? They can be people you know, people you see in the media, or religious or cultural groups.

2. Choose someone you think would be "hard to sell" on hearing about Jesus. Set aside time today to specifically pray that before you reach the end of this book, God will give you an opportunity to talk about Jesus with them in a way they will be excited about and will engage in gladly.

CHAPTER 4

DISCERNING THE GOOD NEWS

The Importance of Learning to Listen

THEY USED TO CALL ME "DR. LOVE."

It's not what it sounds like. I was, in fact, relatively terrible in my relationships with the ladies for most of my single life. I certainly did not receive a doctorate in loveology.

My wife, Krista, and I—along with our friend Nicole— used to spend a lot of time with college students: getting into their lives, getting to know them, and talking about spiritual things. One fun activity we started was going into dorms for "hosted conversations" about relationships. It was called "Dr. Love," and the whole idea was to talk about relationships and teach interpersonal skills in a workshop setting. It was goofy, funny, and quite popular.

During one of our Dr. Love seminars, a kid in the back named Tyrone seemed less connected, less interested, and less interactive than everyone else. He perked up a little when we talked about certain things (like dealing with depression), but complete disinterest set in when we were on topics like "How to Know if You're in Love" or "Finding a Compatible Partner." He seemed more engaged when we talked about dealing with a breakup, but even then, his attention seemed, well . . . sort of sideways.

We were there to build relationships, and yes, we definitely were hoping to share the good news with people like Tyrone, shoud opportunities arise. In the meantime, we gave some relationship advice that came from the Bible, and we always talked about the importance of having spiritual conversations with your partner.

All our conversations were built around this assumption that good news for these kids would be related to the question "How can I have a successful, fulfilling relationship?" But that wasn't true for Tyrone. He didn't seem to care.

During a get-to-know-you section of Dr. Love, one of the questions was "What do you do with your free time?" Tyrone shared that he volunteered at a suicide prevention hotline. We asked him why.

"Because about a year ago, my girlfriend committed suicide," he said.

And with that, Dr. Love was done. Our goofy, funny, popular little presentation seized up and ended. It wasn't fun or entertaining anymore. I sat to talk with Tyrone, and the rest of the students chatted quietly with one another as they went back to their rooms.

Learning to Listen

We made some assumptions about the people in the room when we did "Dr. Love." They were pretty fair, easy assumptions: that people coming to our relationships workshops were interested in talking about relationships, for instance. But in trying to connect with Tyrone's needs about relationships, we were missing the mark. He wanted to talk about grief and loss because of a previous relationship. That's pretty different. If we had done a straight-out lecture, we would have never had this insight . . . or at least not in the context of our presentation. "You can have healthy relationships" wasn't good news for Tyrone, or at least not compelling enough to overcome his greater need. "You can have true healing," though, was good news that could draw him toward Jesus and the universal good news.

We need to figure out how to get into people's lives enough to know their personal needs, so we can share the personal good news they'll find most compelling. Following are five things to remember as you start spiritual conversations with people.

Ask questions.

Let people share where they are in life. You don't have to guess what their needs are—just ask them. It's important when you're asking questions, too, to make sure you're truly listening. Don't spend time thinking about what you want to say in response, or how to connect this to the good news, or what your next question will be. Be present and listen to their answers. Most people will reciprocate with questions of their own in time. It's okay sometimes to wait to be asked a question rather than pushing your statements into the conversation.

I know a guy named Doug who is masterful at this. He has a way of asking questions that get to a person's heart. He was a youth pastor when I worked with him, and I remember when a mom of one of the high schoolers pulled Doug into his office and yelled and screamed at him. He didn't deserve it, but he didn't get angry or start yelling back. He just calmly asked her, "Are you okay? I can tell you're bitter about something. Would you like to talk about it?" She stopped yelling, burst into tears, sat down in front of his desk, and shared what was going on in her life.

Build a relationship, not an agenda.

Have you ever met one of those people who sees you as either a project or a stepping stone? You know, the guy who wants to connect because you're friends with Taylor Swift? Or the lady who keeps inviting you over and just happens to mention how great her ionized water filter is, and did she mention that she sells them? Or, you know, the missionary who wants to come over to talk, but what they really want is for you to add fifty dollars a month to their support. (As a supported missionary,

I'd suggest you ignore the first two . . . but I'd like to come over to your place and talk about the third one.)

Most of us can sense ulterior motives, which means that we need to *not* have ulterior motives when it comes to sharing the good news. You don't make friends so you can share the good news; you make friends because they are people you care about and want to get to know . . . and you share the good news because they are your friends.

Take your time—the good news often starts out small.

The good news is a seed. You don't have to plant a forty-foot maple in the first conversation. Maybe you're only going to get to "God loves you." Or maybe you don't even get that far! Maybe you'll just get to "I believe there is a God." If you're going to be in relationship with this person, you're going to have opportunities to move the conversation forward in the weeks, months, and years to come.

Ah, but what if he or she is a stranger, or someone you know you won't see again? Two things to remember: One, most people like new friends. It's okay to say, "Hey, I really enjoyed this conversation. How can we stay in touch?" Two, God isn't going to lose track of this person. Maybe you'll plant the seed, and someone else will water it. But it is God who makes the seed grow.[1]

Put people before presentation.

What if, when Tyrone told us about his girlfriend, I had said, "Well, that's sad, Tyrone, but we're here to talk about getting new girlfriends and boyfriends." That would have been both insensitive and terrible. Sometimes we get so focused on telling people about Jesus right now that we end up trampling on what they're trying to say to us. Sometimes, like with Tyrone, it's even the deep hurt that might lead them to understand the good news about a loving God who brings life. Remember this: Evangelism is always, always, always about people. We have to learn to see people before we can share with them.

Ask permission to go deeper.

Sometimes we are so eager to push our spiritual conversations to the next place that we can scarcely contain ourselves. Our friend says, "Hey, I got some good news today!" and we burst out, "Is it about how God loves the world and sent his only Son?" That's not bad—it's great to be excited. But asking for permission to talk about deeper things shows a lot of respect for your communication partner.

So, for instance, when Tyrone shared about his girlfriend, it would have been so simple to ask a question like "What do you think happens after you die?" (That's not, incidentally, a bad question at all . . . it could be a great way to transition to that conversation.) It shows so much more respect and care, though, to ask a question like "Tyrone, this is such a painful and important part of your life. I'd like to talk about spiritual things with you. Would that be okay?" Then Tyrone gets to choose whether he wants to walk into that conversation, and he knows that if he wants out of the conversation, you're going to respect him and his boundaries.

This deepening relationship starts to do a variety of things. Someone like Tyrone, for example, starts to experience the good news through your care, kindness, and questions. Believe it or not, it's rare to find loving people when you are in the midst of crisis and trauma. Also, you start to get insight into the sort of person Tyrone is and what his needs and questions are. You start to understand what *his* gospel is: the good news about Jesus that he will find most compelling. And that is going to take us to the place where we're ready to initiate with the most important message Tyrone will ever hear in his life.

So now we've talked about what the gospel is, how to know the universal good news, and how to discover someone's personal good news. Now we need to explore how to communicate that good news in a participatory way that allows someone like Tyrone to hear and respond to the good news . . . and allows us to make sure he's both hearing and understanding.

Reflection Questions

1. Have you ever tried to say something important, only to be brushed aside because someone was busy or had

some other objective in the conversation? How did that make you feel? How can you avoid making others feel that way when sharing the good news?

2. How would your gospel conversations change if you knew for a fact you would be friends with someone and relationally connected for ten minutes? Ten hours? Ten months? Ten years?

3. What do you think about the statement "The good news often starts out small"? Is that true or not in your experience? If it is true, what are the ramifications for us in our gospel conversations? Likewise, if it isn't true, how would that affect our conversations?

4. Which is more difficult or frightening for you—sharing Christ with a stranger or sharing Christ with a close friend or family member?

Exercises

1. Start a conversation with someone this week where you try to ask five questions for every statement you make. Make sure the questions are appropriate and show real interest in the person, but do your best to keep the focus on them, not on you.

2. Pick someone you're already friends with who doesn't know Jesus. Send them a text saying, "I'd like to get together sometime and hear how you're doing."

Then focus on building a trusting, safe conversation where they can truly share their life and heartaches. If appropriate, ask them how you can help or for permission to pray for them.

CHAPTER 5

CAN YOU HEAR ME?

Communication and the Good News

IN OUR CULTURE, whether you are an atheist, a fundamentalist Christian, a Muslim, or a Buddhist, you probably have an opinion about Jesus. That's why, when I was asked to speak at a college outreach on the East Coast, I decided to talk about our different perceptions of Jesus and how we can examine them to discover if they are true.

One thing I shared was that I believed anyone could follow Jesus, that every single person in the audience was loved by God, that each one of them was valuable and important as a human being. And if they wanted a relationship with God, all they had to do was say so and move toward him. This is our message, right? The good news.

Afterward, a young man pulled me aside. We'll call him Mark. He had a defiant look on his face, and I could tell he was looking for a fight. "Can *I* follow Jesus?" Mark asked. His tone was sarcastic, and he had a fierce, almost mocking look on his face.

"Of course you can," I said.

Mark smiled as if I had walked into a trap. With a flourish, he pulled up his sleeve, revealing a rainbow-colored wristband. "I'm the LGBT Student Alliance president," he said. "Now do you think I can follow Jesus?"

I laughed, and without pausing for a second, I said, "Of course you can."

The triumphant look on his face disappeared, replaced with a look of real fear. He thought I would say no and we would have a fight, and then he would call me homophobic and maybe write an opinion article for the school newspaper.

"Let's talk about how you can follow Jesus," I said, but he was already backing away. This was unexpected, dangerous territory.

He couldn't escape now, though. He was the one who asked the question, and I was determined to give him an answer in language he could understand.

Now What?

Most of us have this fantasy where someone we want to talk to about Jesus walks up and says, "Can you tell me how to be saved?" It doesn't happen often (I've seen it maybe twice), but there's this hope someone will want to hear the good news and respond. But honestly, if that happened, you might end up unsure what to say.

If *everyone wants to hear good news*, and we spend time trying to discern what that good news might be for someone, the next question would be, Well, how do we tell them? We have a clear idea of this wonderful, beautiful *message* we call the good news. We know the universal good news, and we have some idea how to uncover their personal good news. How do we make sure they hear what we're trying to say?

It's a more important question than we might realize, because—and we've all experienced this—communication is rarely uncomplicated. How many times have you found yourself in the middle of a conversation and wondering, *Wait, how did we get here?*

Earlier tonight, I was texting with one of my best friends, and we had a major miss. We were both trying to say nice things to each other, but we ended the conversation frustrated and upset because what we were saying wasn't getting across.

My eight-year-old, at least once a day, throws up her hands and says, "Dad! You don't understand!"

In an earlier draft of this book, I went crazy and started putting in diagrams and explanations and gave a sort of crash course on communication theory and how it works. Every single reader said, "I'm just not getting this clearly." It was so clear and beautiful in my head (and I had diagrams!), but somehow it wasn't getting from me (the author) to them (the readers).

Remember that ridiculous game called "Telephone"? That's the one where you whisper to your friend, "My uncle wants a house with an island view," and she whispers to the person next to her the same message, and so on around the circle until it comes back to you as "A knuckle with a mouse says I love you."

Our messages, whether casual or challenging, can go off track just as easily. So with something as important, simple, and yet complex as the good news, how do I make sure my message gets transmitted from me to you without getting corrupted, misunderstood, or misheard? To answer that, let's go back to Mark from earlier in the chapter.

After a disastrous attempt to lay a trap for me, Mark has just accidentally opened himself up to hearing the good news. I am gleefully delighted. Mark is wary and nervous. I know, more or less, my message. But how do I get it across to Mark so that he hears and understands?

In this scenario, I am obviously the messenger. But communication, as we all know, is not a one-way street. It is a complicated intersection with high-speed traffic, lights that keep changing, and slightly confusing street signs. So while I may be the messenger, Mark is going to be my communication partner. I'm getting a message to him, but he has to participate in the process.

As the messenger, though, I get to initiate. So I need to decide my mode of communication (which we'll call our *signal*), and I need to figure out how to get what is in my head *translated* into that signal and over to Mark.

Since Mark is right in front of me, my signal doesn't have to be complicated. I'm not going to text him (although my high schoolers might do that from the same room). I'm not going to send him an email, or Snapchat him, or use semaphore. In this situation, I'm going to speak to him. Easy decision. So I say to Mark, out loud with my voice, "Mark, you can follow Jesus."

Mark, my partner in this whole communication thing, has to take my message and see if he can translate exactly what I mean. If he can, my message was understandable and correctly received. Now as it happens, Mark *doesn't* exactly understand what I am saying. I can tell, because he reiterates back to me, "But I'm gay."

See, I already knew that. Mark made that pretty clear with the whole rainbow wristband and announcement of his role as president of the LGBT Student Alliance. Something is blocking my message from being received. Perhaps some people in Mark's life have made it clear that he's not welcome in church or the presence of God.

Since he's not understanding my message, I need to adjust it a little. I have to say the same thing but say it another way: "Mark, what I'm trying to say to you is that God loves gay people. Jesus loves gay people." What's beautiful here is that this is both the universal good news ("God loved the world so much . . .") and the personal ("Yes, that includes you").

Mark is starting to understand the message . . . his eyes widen. He doesn't believe it, not yet, but he is hearing and understanding, maybe for the first time, the good news.

Mark's next question (and maybe yours, too) is whether I think it's a sin to be gay, or at least to live an actively gay life-style. So let's pause for a moment and remind ourselves who Mark is: a college student who is a leader on campus and has had some unloving, unkind interactions with our brothers and sisters in the church, to the point that he thought God didn't love him.

Think about that. Our communication to him, as the church, left him believing our "good news" is that the most powerful being in the universe disapproves of and possibly hates him. He flinches when he sees another student with a cross tattoo on his arm. His jaw tightens when he drives by a church. He goes to his uncle's funeral, and the whole time he's sitting in the pew, all he can think is, *Every person in this place is judging me.*

And my job, in this moment, is to bring him the good news about Jesus.

The good news—the great news—is that Mark doesn't need an answer to this question in order to come to Jesus. Maybe someone else in a similar situation would, but not Mark.

"Mark, do you want to be in a relationship with Jesus?"

He thinks about this. "Yeah. I didn't think I was allowed to, but yeah."

And that's sufficient. We can go from there. He's heard the message. The good news has come through loud and clear.

That's not the end of our conversation, of course. God's good news always continues. Maybe the next part of our conversation is something like "You've messed up, and you have these broken places in your life. Do you want healing from that? Do you want forgiveness? Do you want a way to be in deep relationship with God? Then I have great, great news for you: Jesus came and died and rose again, and you can have all those things."

We don't have to catalog every sin Mark has ever done or is doing. Mark doesn't have to fix himself and jettison all his sins before coming to Jesus. He needs to bring those to Jesus, not fix himself up and then come to Jesus. Those sins that are unclear or confusing or that he's unaware of . . . well, the Holy Spirit will make them clear in time.

"But," you might say, "Mark is still a sinner!" Well, yeah. Me too. After all these years of following Jesus, being a missionary, writing Christian books, and going to church for decades, I'm still a sinner. I'm not the only one, I trust. I have a hunch you are too.

While we were still sinners, Christ died for us. That's good news. *We love him because he first loved us.* That's good news. *God delights to show mercy.* Ah, thank God. That is good news indeed.[1]

Communication and the Signal

Whatever mode of communication we use, whatever our signal, the goal is the same: for you and me, the messengers, to take the message in our hearts and deliver it to the people we're talking to. Mark and I chose the spoken word as our signal, our mode of communication. But it's important to be aware of how many signals we have access to, how many ways we can be intentional in making sure our message gets heard. For example, face-to-face communication isn't limited to just talking; it's full of other "signals" too: Tone of voice. Body language. The speed of our words, and whether we cut others off or listen to them. Whether or not we ask questions, and whether we seem to really care about the answers. How often we check our phones or watches.

Paying attention to all these different signals and how we use them will help us in our process. Keeping an eye on all the different ways we're communicating will help us be more clear and move more quickly from our initial communication to understanding one another.

Any conversation will likely follow this process: You communicate something, and the other person responds; you realize you didn't quite get your message across, and you try again with an adjusted message or a new signal. Hopefully you keep going until you're both confident you're understanding each other.

This is the basic rhythm of communication, sending an intended message through a signal and translating the meaning until the message is heard. We see God entering the communication cycle in just this way in the book of Jeremiah. He has just chosen the young man, and he sends him a vision. "What do you see, Jeremiah?" he asks. So at this point, God has a message, has translated it, and has sent it through a vision—the signal.

Jeremiah replies that he sees "the branch of an almond tree." So Jeremiah receives the signal, translates it, and reflects it back through his own communication.

"You have seen correctly," God says, then explains what the almond branch means (it's a pun—"almond tree" sounds like "watching" in Hebrew—and God says Jeremiah has seen correctly because God is watching to make sure his Word is fulfilled). Then he goes through the process a second time with a second vision.[2]

In this story, God is checking the communication process. He's making sure his message is coming through clearly by entering into the communication cycle with Jeremiah. Since we are made in the image of God, we need to follow his example. We need to make sure we're intentional about our communication, checking the signal for each person we talk to, in order to make sure they're receiving the right message and understanding it in the most accurate way based on how they interpret things.

After a conversation with someone like Mark, we might follow up via a different signal: with an email, a text, a phone call, or, I don't know, a music video. But as good messengers, what we'll always do is enter the cycle, making sure the message is clear to our partners.

Did Mark pray to receive Jesus after our conversations? No.

But he heard and understood the good news.

And I hope the next time Mark sees a student with a cross tattoo, he's reminded, maybe only for a moment, of our conversation about a God who loves him and died so that he can live.

Reflection Questions

1. How would you have shared the good news about Jesus with Mark?

2. If someone came up to you and asked, "What do I have to do to be saved?" what would you say to them? What method would you use? How would you make sure they were following your message?

3. Can you think of a time when changing the words you used might have changed the way a conversation went?

Exercises

1. Watch for the communication cycle today in your interactions with others. How many times do you have to cycle back around and clarify or say things a different way to get to the intended meaning? How does the complexity of the discussion topic affect things? How about the relationship (or lack thereof) with your communication partner—how does that affect things?

2. Take a common communication in your everyday life and try it in a new way. In other words, if you always call a loved one to say hello once a week, try writing a letter instead. If you text your friend to say hi every day, try calling them. Or rather than sending your friend a note on social media, drop by and see them in person.

CHAPTER 6

THE GOSPEL ACCORDING TO TWILIGHT SPARKLE

Creating Fluent Translations of the Good News

MY KIDS HAVE ALL GONE to Bible club for years. It meets weekly, and the kids memorize Bible verses, play games, and hang out with their friends. They love it, and they've learned a lot.

A while back, I happened to be there when one of the staff gave a gospel presentation. It was during a big "game day," and at "halftime," someone took the stage to talk about Jesus.

The first thing he did was choose seven kids from the audience and put them onstage with big signs that had cartoon figures on them, each meant to represent something about the good news. So far so good.

This staff person, who was probably in his early seventies, got the kids' attention and said to them, "I want to go to heaven. I have an artificial hip and a fake knee, and I can't wait to get a new body."

That's interesting.

Because that is absolutely good news about Jesus: In the coming Kingdom, he will do away with death, and we will have new, healed bodies. But these were seven- and eight-year-olds. They all appeared to have functional bodies and weren't in imminent need of repairs.

That comment just washed over the kids.

Then he turned to the seven kids onstage. Each one had a word or phrase they were meant to shout after he said something to them. So he would say to the first kid, "Jesus provides salvation for all," and the kid would shout, "GLORY!" and then the audience was meant to shout, "GLORY!"—which isn't terrible, right? We have participation from the kids, the audience shouting, and a lot of repetition (an essential part of oral communication, especially if you want people to remember things), because when he moved on to the second kid's key word, he would repeat the first.

So it went like this:

"Jesus provides salvation for all."
"GLORY!"
"Is everyone a sinner?"
"WE ARE ALL LOST!"
"And what is the penalty of our sins?"
"WE HAVE FALLEN SHORT OF GOD'S GLORY!"

And so on, through seven kids. When he reached the end, he said to the kids, "Let's recite John 3:16 together." These are mostly kids who go to Bible club every week, so that wasn't a strange request. All these kids know John 3:16.

But then he did the weirdest thing.

He said—and I am not kidding, these were his actual words—"I know all you children have learned this verse in the NIV, but I prefer the King James Version, so I am going to recite it in the King James."

Strange, since the kids all knew the NIV translation. So he said *begotten* and *whosoever* and *believeth* into the microphone while the kids stumbled along in their version.

Now, the good news is effectual because the Holy Spirit makes it so. Kids can come to know Jesus through a gospel presentation like this one, and I know kids have become followers of Jesus through identical presentations.

But it's unfortunate that this godly man who loves kids didn't want to participate *more* with the kids in this presentation. The John 3:16 thing in particular makes me sad, because he said he knew the kids had memorized it in another version, but *he was going to stick with his preference.* This reveals that at some level, he wasn't committed to doing a gospel presentation for the kids—he was committed to doing "his" gospel presentation.

And that explains why he started out by talking about how lame it is to have a body that's falling apart and how he wished he could get to heaven and have a new body. This gentleman had contextualized and translated the good news about Jesus, but he had contextualized and translated it *to himself* rather than for the kids.

Now, that conclusion isn't completely fair, because he had included some great things the kids loved—the call and response, the audience participation, the signs with the cartoons. But those things are all *signals*, the modes by which he transmitted the message. He had chosen compelling signals for his audience, but he hadn't translated his message for them.

To See and Know

Good communication requires that we see and know the receiving partner of our communication. Scripture is jammed full of stories where Jesus (or his followers) share good news in a way specifically tailored to the person receiving the good news.

Imagine if evangelism were done without seeing or knowing those communication partners, though. For instance, think about when Peter and John were on their way to pray at the Temple. As they approached the gate, a crippled man called out to them, asking for money.[1] But what if they had been in a hurry and hadn't bothered to stop and see what his needs were? And what if instead they'd rolled out a version of the good news they had used earlier in the week with someone who had been caught in adultery? "God wants you to only have sex with your spouse. But you have been forgiven! Go your way and sin no more." We could forgive the poor, crippled beggar for not understanding how this is good news.

(And it is wonderful news! He just might not see how it has to do with him.)

But that's not what happened in this story. Peter and John did stop and look at the man. They saw he was begging for money because he was unable to work. In fact, they saw a problem greater than the one for which he had asked for help. He needed money, but the real issue was deeper: He needed money because his physical maladies prevented him from making a living.

So Peter said, "We don't have any money, but we do have something to give you. In the name of Jesus Christ of Nazareth, get up and walk."[2] That was good news the man could understand. So he jumped to his feet and ran around and leaped off things and shouted his brand-new good news about God.[3]

In this particular instance, Peter and John didn't share their own personal good news ("I was a fisherman," Peter might say, "and Jesus healed my mother-in-law and then taught me to catch fish"), though they do that elsewhere. Instead, they

1. stopped what they were doing,
2. looked at the man and his needs, and
3. shared good news that directly addressed those needs.

They saw him and knew him, and they participated with the Holy Spirit not only in sharing the gospel but also in providing good news through his healing.

With this in mind, I might have a different approach than telling a seven-year-old about my aches and pains if I were sharing good news with them. What is good news about Jesus for a seven-year-old child?

Well, most of us have been kids and have some idea. For me personally, I remember stumbling across a book called *The Gospel according to Star Wars* as a kid. I went crazy for it and read that thing cover to cover. I didn't understand it all, but I loved it, and it changed the way I watched *Star Wars*. (I had already worn a VHS tape nearly to destruction, watching it over and over.) More than lightsabers, though—and definitely more than aching joints or old bones—most kids want safety and to know they're loved, which can be great places to start when it comes to the good news.

Here's the thing: Most of us know how to speak to kids. We know how to simplify our language and speak to their concerns. When I have a message for a child, I know how to contextualize my message so they can partner well and understand what I am saying.

So while we could spend some time in this chapter crafting the perfect gospel presentation for a child, I think we're ready for a challenge. Let's take it up a notch, maybe go a little bit crazy. Let's talk about *My Little Pony*.

My Little Brony

Have you heard of "Bronies"? The Brony movement started when adult males realized they loved the children's cartoon

My Little Pony. The cartoon is a sweet, fun show about multicolored ponies (and unicorns! and winged ponies! and "Alicorns"!) who live in a magic land and have adventures revolving around questions of friendship and kindness. It's designed to sell toys, and many kids—regardless of gender— love it.

The "Bronies" are adult men who enjoy the cartoon. Maybe some are fathers who started watching it with their kids, or college students whose only break in the afternoon came at the same time the show did. Regardless, these men loved the cartoon when they discovered it and eventually found one another online and started a community.

I've met some Bronies, and most of them legitimately just enjoy the cartoon, like talking about it, and find the community to be inclusive, kind, and loving. (In fact, the Brony movement now includes adults of any gender who love the show. I've even met little kids who call themselves Bronies. It's come to mean, in some contexts, anyone who loves the show.) It's not much different, honestly, than adult *Star Wars* fans who love to collect *Star Wars* toys or watch the cartoon *Star Wars Rebels.*

Now, imagine you have an acquaintance or a relative who is a Brony.[4] He's named Brock, he's twenty-six, and he has felt socially isolated for a long time—but he's really found joy in the show and acceptance in the Brony community. Brock has a picture of Rainbow Dash in his wallet, and whenever you walk by the produce section, he says something about Applejack. He also has a little purple dragon on the dash of his car.

Brock is not opposed to spiritual things, but he doesn't perk up when you talk about them, either. Most of his friends are online, and you know he's longing for real community here in your hometown.

You really want to talk to him about Jesus.

So you

1. stop what you're doing,
2. look at Brock and his needs, and
3. share *Brock's good news* about Jesus with him.

The first step, stopping what you're doing, is pretty easy. You just need to spend a little time thinking about Brock. You care about the guy, so it's not a big deal to set aside ten minutes or half an hour to just focus on what you know about him.

The second step, looking at Brock, reveals you already see a pretty easy way to talk about the good news with the guy. He is longing for deeper connections in community, and that's absolutely part of the good news. God didn't intend for people to be alone, and entering the community of faith is described as being adopted into a family. There's a lot there Brock will love.

Now, when it comes to sharing the good news with Brock, there are some great options:

1. You could just sit down with him and walk through a "generic" gospel presentation. You could tell him

how you want to go to heaven because your knees hurt, and then throw jargon at him and quote from the King James Bible as you explain that God loves Brock—we're all broken; God wants to be in relationship with human beings; and Jesus died and rose again so Brock could be with him. Something like that. I believe the Holy Spirit would honor that, and although you weren't doing much translation (You were doing some—you used Brock's name and explained the Bible verses and jargon along the way!), God would speak to his heart.

2. You could start with the need Brock has, just like Peter and John did with the crippled beggar. You could talk about how God brings us into community and family; how that has worked for you—the rich relationships you have at church or with other believers—and how you're inviting him into that community. Again, of course, you would get to Jesus being God, and sin and forgiveness and resurrection, but you would use Brock's needs as the starting point. God could speak to Brock in that, and the conversation would be more engaging, more memorable, less awkward, and less about your being the "teacher" and more about your coming alongside him as a friend.

Or . . .

3. You could go full-on Brony.

Twilight Sparkle's Good News

I lived in Asia for several years, and I vividly remember returning to the States to see an American who had gotten a Chinese character tattooed on his arm.

I asked him, "Why did you choose that character?"

"It's the character for *love*," he said.

But it wasn't. It was the character for *water*.

Maybe he loved water . . . but I suspect he didn't know enough Chinese to realize the translation was incorrect.

If you want to translate something, you need to speak at least two languages. So if we want to get truly involved in translating the good news into Brock's language, we should get to know the language, jargon, culture, and interests of his community, the Bronies, so we can more fluently translate our message into Brony language.

Don't worry. I'm not about to spend an entire chapter teaching you all about Bronies so you can share Christ with them. What I did, though, was spend a little time talking to a few Bronies and looking at a website called whatisabrony.com. Why? To get to know their culture and what matters to them so I could figure out how the gospel intersects with the Brony world.

As I got to know the Bronies, I noticed they were quite spiritual, and indeed, a basic concern with moral action is at their core. Community and the desire for healthy, beautiful friendships is by far the deepest value of the *My Little Pony* world, and in fact, the *My Little Pony* slogan is "Friendship is Magic."

The cartoon revolves around this idea that there is an unbreakable bond that allows even evil creatures to be redeemed and enter into community with the ponies. There is also something called "the Elements of Harmony," which is key to living a good life: honesty, kindness, laughter, generosity, loyalty, and magic. (And remember, magic is actually the power of friendship.)

Now get ready for this. Here's the good news I might share with Brock:

> Brock, human beings are like Discord . . . we've betrayed God. God wants us to be his friends, and like Twilight Sparkle, he's willing to save us from evil like Tirek so we can be together in Equestria. None of us perfectly follow the Elements of Harmony— we have been dishonest, disloyal, or unkind.
>
> But the power of God's friendship is so strong that he sent Jesus. Just like Twilight Sparkle came on behalf of Celestia, and she gave up all her magic to save the ponies . . . Jesus also gave up his power—and even his life!—to save us. He did this so we could be in community with God and each other, and just like Twilight Sparkle got her magic back, Jesus came back to life and showed he had power over everything . . . even the evils of disharmony and disloyalty and creatures like Tirek.
>
> And even though you have been fighting God, like Discord fought the ponies, you can be brought into

real friendship with him . . . because God's friendship is magic. Like Discord, you have to apologize and admit you've been a terrible friend. But God is loyal, honest, kind, and generous, and he brings joy. He is, in fact, the greatest source of harmony in the universe.

If I did my job right, that previous paragraph should be almost incomprehensible to you unless you're a Brony. Because the good news of Jesus (which is in that paragraph, I promise) *wasn't translated for you*. But a Brony should be able to not only hear the good news in this but also immediately latch on to the meaning without much explanation on my part. It's possible I've missed some nuances here because I'm not "fluent" in Brony. But with a little work on my end, I can participate more deeply with God in sharing the good news, *and* I can shoulder the more difficult and confusing parts of communication rather than expecting Brock to do so.

I can't keep myself from sharing this, too: Twilight Sparkle, after she saves all the ponies, tells them she realizes her mission is to "spread the magic of friendship across Equestria"— which is a pretty easy way to explain the great commission to Brock, should he choose to come into the community of friendship with the great and loving God.

Can We Take This Too Far?

You may feel I've gone too far in the last example. The discomfort, confusion, or concern you may feel is *not* because the gospel isn't clear in "The Good News of Twilight

Sparkle"—it's because it isn't clear *to you*. But that's because you're not fluent in Brony.

So let me ask you this. Is the following sentence part of the good news?

"耶稣爱你."

If you read a little Chinese, then you recognize these simple characters immediately. They say, "Jesus [耶稣] loves [爱] you [你]." But if you don't read Chinese, you wouldn't have known the difference had I written, "耶稣水你," which is a nonsense sentence that says, "Jesus water you."

Remember, translation requires understanding two languages. If you don't understand both languages, you can't make a good determination as to whether a translation is a good one. But I promise that Brony translation is a decent one, and it includes "you're a sinner" as well as "God loves you and died for you" and "you must repent and turn to God."

This is what the apostle Paul was getting at when he said he became "all things to all people so that by all possible means [he] might save some."[5] He wasn't saying he would just keep repeating things in the same way no matter who he was talking to. Paul was sharing the good news just like Jesus did—and Jesus radically altered how he talked about the good news based on his audience (which we'll look at in detail in the next chapter!).

In my experience, most Christians today are far, far away from the "too far" line in contextualizing the good news and much closer to the "not communicating clearly" side of things.

But it is a fair question to ask: How can we tell if we've gone too far? Is it possible we could go so far toward "translating" the good news that we corrupt it? How can we tell if we've gone too far?

Here are three suggested guidelines to explore when you're wondering if you're "translating" appropriately:

1. Make sure your standard of success is whether the communication is clear *to the communication partner receiving the message.*

    Don't worry about someone outside that audience who doesn't understand it. It's *not* a problem if our message is unclear to those who are not our intended audience. Sometimes well-meaning religious people will critique contextualized explanations of the good news because they don't understand them. The message wasn't for them, so they think it's corrupted good news when really it's just not in their language.

    Bible translators sometimes run into this. Let's say you're a Wycliffe Bible translator working with a remote tribe who doesn't have ice or refrigerators—and has never seen those things either. If you wanted to communicate that "the blood of Christ will make you white as snow,"[6] how would you do it?

    Well, just like with jargon, you could explain it to them—you could invent a word for *snow* in their language, then explain to them what snow is, and then tell them snow is pure white. Or you could try to find things in their culture that fit the description—so your translation might say "as white as bleached cloth."

If you're like me, this might freak you out a little bit. But remember, our English Bible translations already do this. For instance, if your English Bible never says someone "covered their feet," it's because your translation is helping you understand what is *meant* rather than what the words in Scripture *actually say*. In ancient times, to cover your feet meant to drop your robe to use the restroom. So your Bible might say "relieved himself" instead. It switches out the culturally relevant metaphor from the past with a contemporary one. This is largely considered an appropriate means of communication and translation (though there are those who fight about it).

Let's take it a little further. Maybe this same tribe doesn't have sheep, so the term *Lamb of God* is complete nonsense. But they do have pigs. After some intense argument and study, you decide *Pig of God* mostly makes sense: These are animals used in sacrifice in their culture. And when you try the phrase out on some tribal people, they seem to immediately, almost intuitively, understand: "Ah, like a pig, Jesus died so I could be forgiven and enter into God's good graces." So it's working.

Missionary translators probably don't want to start talking about the "Pig of God" in the United States, because people would think they were corrupting the good news . . . but to the tribal people, it's perfectly clear and makes more gospel sense than "Lamb of God."

It's wise to get feedback and critiques from others as you're doing these things, but don't let someone judge your translation if they're not moving toward fluency in the same language. Often the best judge of your translation will be a new believer (or nonbeliever!) in the context you're trying to reach.

2. Ask yourself, *Does my "translation" require sinful or evil actions?*

I read an article a few years ago about a married couple who were reaching out to the "swingers" community to share Jesus with them. Swingers are usually married couples who have sexual relationships with one another's spouses. It's a sort of "free love" movement. This couple decided the best way to reach out to that community was to participate in it. They "used swinging" as a way to share the gospel, complete with sexual immorality.

I don't know these people and whether they were truly Christ followers who had lost their way, or what. I do know this: *Participating in sinful actions as an example of the good news is crossing a line* that Jesus and his followers in Scripture did not ever cross.

Did Jesus sometimes trample all over legalism to share the good news? Sure. People accused him of being a drunkard and a glutton because he attended parties with gluttons and drunkards. Jesus sometimes allowed himself to look bad to share the good news, but he never sinned to share it.

Same with Paul—he was accused of sin by the Jews because of the way he interacted with non-Jews when he shared the good news (for instance, he didn't avoid eating with non-Jews[7]), but he wasn't sinning. The Jews misunderstood what he was doing (and he did his best to live like a Jew among the Jews and a Greek among the Greeks[8]). This required some sophisticated cultural awareness, but Paul worked hard not to cross this line and was—so far as we know from Scripture—largely successful.

3. Ask yourself, *Am I going beyond my fluency in my communication partner's language?*

If you're not sure what you're communicating, then "translating" becomes about as useful as not translating. It's better to keep it simple and understandable than to get complicated and confuse someone. Of course, the Holy Spirit is there, translating alongside you, but why make things messier than they should be?

For instance, my "Pony Gospel" was created without full fluency. I've seen a couple episodes of *My Little Pony* with my daughters. My sisters liked it when I was a kid. And like I mentioned, I know a couple Bronies, and I read some articles online.

But to get truly fluent, I need to spend more time with native speakers. I should hang out with a Brony and try out my Brony good news. I need his feedback, and I need to see if he understands what's being said. As Mark Twain said, there's a pretty big difference between lightning and a lightning bug. When you're communicating beyond your fluency level, you're likely to make some mistakes.

A really good explanation of the good news is going to be different for different people. We'll use different words, different approaches, and new metaphors, and we'll talk about the Bible differently—maybe we'll use different translations or just paraphrase without pulling a Bible out at all, or we'll write a few words on a napkin.

That's because there's a difference between a seven-year-old and a seventy-year-old in life experience, understanding, and language. Millennials and boomers look at the world differently. An African American woman raised in the upper middle class of New York City has a different language than a white guy who has lived his entire life in a mobile home in Texas. Juggalos and Beliebers don't understand each other or have the same value sets. The woman next to me on the plane who is learning English and the newlywed couple from Michigan sitting across the aisle all want to hear good news, but where we start and how we talk about it is going to be different.

In the end, the point is this: People should be respected, and if we're going to share with them the most important message of their lives, it's only respectful to get to know them and the way they speak and feel and look at the world as we share that message.

Reflection Questions

1. How did you feel about the good news of Twilight Sparkle? What made sense to you? What was confusing? What made you nervous or uncomfortable? Did it seem like a legitimate presentation of the good news?

2. Think back on how you first heard the story of Jesus, and think about the person who was your messenger. How difficult do you think it was for them to say things in a way that made sense to you?

3. Do you have a preferred way to talk to people about Jesus? For example, a tool you like to use, or a way you like to start a conversation (or maybe you wait for them to bring it up). Or perhaps you like to show a certain movie or have people over for dinner. Would you be willing to give up your preferred way—even

if it was uncomfortable for you—if it would make the good news clearer to people with whom you share it?

Exercises

1. Choose a people group you don't know much about and do some research into their culture. Make a list of specific things you would do and say to translate the good news to them more clearly. Choose a group that interests you, or maybe there's someone in your life whom you've been wanting to understand better. If you're having trouble coming up with ideas, choose one of these groups:

   - the Roma people in the United States
   - tarot-card readers
   - Roller Derby teams
   - the transgender community
   - second-generation Americans
   - retired people who play bingo every day

2. Ask someone who does not have a church background to help you with this exercise. Tell them you are reading this book and trying to "translate" something from the Bible to people like them, and you need to make sure they completely understand it. Ask if they will help you say it in their words rather than yours. If

you keep this focused on learning about them and the way they say things and communicate, they should enjoy this exercise.

3. This week at church,[9] listen to word choices and observe communications and how things are done. In your opinion, who is the intended audience—"outsiders" or "insiders" to the faith community? If you were going to flip it around, what sorts of changes would you need to make? If you were planning a service specifically for the group you researched in exercise 1 or your friend in exercise 2, how would you do things differently (time of service, music, length of sermon, style, words, decor, location, etc.)?

CHAPTER 7

JESUS THE EVANGELIST

What Is Good News for This Person?

AS I WAS STANDING outside my daughter's grade school, waiting for her to file out so we could go home, two boys came and stood near me. They were about nine. One was skinny and sickly looking, the other round and flushed. The round one held a thick, black leather Bible in his hand, which surprised me because (1) this was a public school, and in my area, you just don't see people walking around holding a Bible, and (2) he had a backpack he could be carrying it in.

The Bible kid leaned over to the other kid and almost whispered, "You're a devil." He looked around furtively. I'm guessing his teacher might have talked to him about this already.

"I am not," the second kid said.

"The Bible says anyone who doesn't believe in God is a devil," Bible kid said, and he held out the book as if to prove it—which would be hard, because that statement is not in there. "You don't believe in God, so you are the devil." The devil!

"I am not!" the second kid said again and moved away from Bible kid. "There's my dad!" He slipped off into the crowd.

Bible kid stood there, watching him go, then murmured, "The devil."

To be honest, I was a little creeped out.

This sort of evangelistic back-and-forth is more common than we'd like to think. Just this morning, I watched an atheist and a Christian spar online.

- **Christian:** You're evil because you don't believe in God.
- *Atheist:* That doesn't make me evil.
- **Christian:** Yes, it does.
- *Atheist:* No, it doesn't.

I wish I were exaggerating, but those are the actual words . . . and they continued from there. No partnership in communication, just two people reaffirming their disagreement with one another.

When we do this, we create an impression that Jesus is the sort of guy who hides behind rocks, his face peeking out, waiting to see you do something evil like smoke a cigarette or use profanity so he can pop out and shout, "AHA!" or maybe, "This is why you're going to hell." And while Jesus did use some pretty strong language, like calling one of his followers Satan,[1] that sort of language seemed to be reserved for people who were already religious and claimed to follow God.

Again, I don't think there's such a thing as a "wrong way" to go about evangelism so long as you aren't harming people, but I do think it's instructive to look at how Jesus did it. We're going to look at two stories about Jesus sharing good news with people (there are many more, but this will give us a good comparison). And we're going to ask some key questions: How did Jesus communicate the good news? How did he interact in these conversations? What can we learn from him?

"Born Again" with Nicodemus

Born again has become such a central metaphor for many in the Christian tradition that it's almost shocking to realize the concept only appears in Scripture a total of four times in two passages (in the story of Nicodemus in John 3:3, 7 and then in 1 Peter 1:3, 23). So it wasn't a "go to" thing Jesus always said to anyone he talked to; it was a phrase he used specifically for Nicodemus.

Take a moment and read the account in John 3:1-21, and be thinking specifically about how Jesus tailored his message (translated it) for Nicodemus.

Nicodemus was a Bible teacher and a member of the

Jewish ruling council. He was an influential man and a leader in the faith community. So it's interesting that Jesus started out not with a theological treatise but by specifically using terminology both unfamiliar and confusing to Nicodemus.

He said Nicodemus must be "born again" (or possibly "born from above"—the Greek could read either way), and we know Nicodemus was confused because he asked, "How can someone be born again? That doesn't make any sense. A person can't climb back inside their mother."[2]

Apparently Nicodemus was a literal thinker and either didn't understand that Jesus was using a metaphor or was so confused by it he asked for clarification.

Now, as an aside, this particular moment might seem like it's arguing against our premise. Jesus was purposely and specifically using communication *not* tailored precisely to Nicodemus. He appeared to be purposely confusing him (although Jesus' saying "You're Israel's teacher and you don't get this?"[3] may suggest Jesus thought it *should have been* obvious what he was saying).

Perhaps Jesus knew diving straight into theology using familiar terms would have allowed Nicodemus to continue "knowing the right answer" and not engage with the paradigm-shattering good news Jesus was about to share. Regardless, when it became clear that Nicodemus, the receiving partner, was not correctly translating the message in the signal, Jesus (1) explained his meaning and (2) used a different translation approach.

In his longer speech, he explained the "being born again"

part: One has to be born physically and of the Spirit (or "from above"). The wind (or "spirit/Spirit"—it's the same word in Greek) blows, and people controlled by the wind/ spirit move along. Jesus knew what he was talking about because he was the one who came from heaven, though he would expect a teacher like Nicodemus to know these things.

Then Jesus shared one sentence that was directly in Nicodemus's language, from a story every Jewish teacher would know in the Scriptures: Moses lifted a snake in the wilderness, and the same thing must be done with the Son of Man, so that anyone who believes in him will live forever.

This was a direct reference to the story in Numbers 21:4-9. The people of Israel had complained against God (in a really funny moment, they both complain they have no bread and complain about the food they're given to eat), and in reply, God sent deadly poisonous snakes to the camp. As people were suffering from snakebites, they repented of their complaints against God and asked Moses to pray for them. God told Moses to make a snake and put it on a pole in the camp. All who looked at the bronze snake wouldn't die from their snakebites.

Jesus was making a comparison that would be plain to a teacher like Nicodemus. God saved the snakebit people of Israel by having Moses put a snake on a pole, and all that was required of the people was a small act of faith: Look to the pole. In the same way, the Messiah was going to be lifted up so the people of the world could be saved . . . if only the people would believe and look to him.

If the "born again" metaphor was unclear to Nicodemus (and it appears it was), Jesus followed up with a comparison that didn't leave much room for confusion, one taken directly from Nicodemus's culture and expertise. Translators disagree whether John 3:16-21 is quoting Jesus or the narrator (the Greek doesn't use quotation marks), but whether it's meant as further explanation for Nicodemus or for the reader doesn't much matter. Either way, it's a continued "translation" of the good news message Jesus brought for Nicodemus: There's a way to live forever with God, whether it's by being "born again" or by looking to the Son of Man lifted up for the world to see.

Notice in this story that Jesus

1. used an approach specific to the person with whom he was interacting,
2. used metaphor and comparison to make spiritual truths more easily understandable,
3. tried a different approach when it was clear his communication partner wasn't receiving the message clearly, and
4. answered Nicodemus's question by starting with his concerns.

"Living Water" with the Woman at the Well

Not much later, in John 4, we see Jesus interact with a completely different sort of person and share the good news in a completely different way. Nicodemus was rich, respected, and a scholar of the Scriptures. The woman Jesus met in chapter 4 was poor and an outcast—and the Jews would have said she was a member of a heretic cult. The Samaritans weren't considered true Jews at all.

Jesus, tired after a long journey, sat by the well outside the city limits while his followers were in town getting food. He couldn't even get himself a drink—as the Samaritan woman pointed out later, it was a deep well, and Jesus didn't have so much as a cup. He had no way to access the cool, fresh water.

Jewish people looked down on Samaritans so much that they would avoid talking to them whenever possible—they would work hard not to look them in the eye and pretend they were invisible. Imagine how many treat homeless people, and you get a decent idea.

So if a Samaritan was drawing water from a well, most Jews would have looked away. And in this case, the person who came out to draw water was, as was typical at the time, a woman. It was scandalous for a godly man to be alone with a woman who wasn't his relative or spouse, and the correct thing for Jesus to do would have been to ignore this woman completely.

And yet—Jesus spoke to her first. He asked her for water. The woman, understandably, thought this was rich coming from a guy who shouldn't even be speaking to her. Of course he'd talk to her if he needed something! She said as much—essentially, "You shouldn't be talking to me at all, but of course you'll break your precious taboos to get something."

Jesus sidestepped this: "As it happens, I have something

even better than what I'm asking you for, and you would have known that if you had known who I am. I asked you for water, but I have *living water*."[4]

This is a fascinating metaphorical moment Jesus provided. In his day, there was a hierarchy of water. If you had to, you'd drink water from a cistern, which had "dead" water—collected runoff water that was still. Drinking it was better than dying of thirst, but cistern water was susceptible to being poisoned and collecting nasty little critters. It was overall inferior to the next level up: well water. Well water was from a running source, but it was underground, hard to access. Still, it was fresh and better than cistern water. The term *living water* was reserved for running water, like a stream or river. Pure, clean, and always moving, living water was the best. So Jesus made a pun here. He was referring to both "running water" and the idea that water could bring life.

The Samaritan woman didn't understand and asked for actual water. Maybe this crazy guy by the well knew something she didn't, knew about some source of water nearby that she, a local, had never heard of. Regardless, it didn't hurt to ask.

Jesus encouraged her to get her husband and come back, but she said she didn't have one. Jesus (supernaturally) told her he was aware of her history. She was amazed and said she could see he was a prophet—and immediately she threw up another objection: the Jews and Samaritans disagree theologically.

Jesus sidestepped her objection again.

Basically, the Samaritan woman was pulling the conversation off center. She was moving it away from Jesus and on to other theological concerns. So Jesus ignored (more or less) those objections and kept moving back to the main point: There was a way for her to experience life with God.

This is interesting because as a kid growing up in church, I was taught to never sidestep objections in evangelistic conversations. I was in high school in the late '80s and '90s, and the number-one topic youth groups loved to tackle at the time was evolution. We watched many videos about evolution versus creation and how to talk to an evolutionist and so on. I had plenty of those conversations, and do you know what? It was rare for a conversation about the fossil record to turn into someone recognizing their need for Jesus.

For most people (not all), that sort of objection is a purposeful evasion of the conversation about Jesus. Whether it's politics, theology, science, or "Is this or that a sin?" people have a way of introducing their own noise to the signal containing the message we're trying to communicate. They ask questions or introduce topics—distractions—that have little to do with the good news.

That's why it's important to watch what Jesus did with this woman. He didn't let the conversation get off track. He sidestepped and then sent the signal again.

Here's the question I ask myself when I'm trying to decide whether to sidestep a question or answer it: Can a person believe this thing and still come into sincere relationship with Jesus? In other words, Would I rather have an evolutionist in heaven or a creationist in hell?

If the conversation we're having doesn't directly affect someone's eternal destination, it might be that it's not the most important part of our conversation. I look at the trajectory and see if it's headed toward Jesus or not. Make no mistake, there are people who need to sort out the question of human origins before coming to Jesus, but in my experience, those people are rare.

When I sidestep this conversation, it might go something like this:

- **Friend:** I can't believe in Jesus because I believe in evolution.
- *Me:* There are many Christians who believe in evolution.
- **Friend:** But I have questions about Christianity. I can't follow Jesus.
- *Me:* You can question Christianity or you can be a Christian with questions, but the core question is what are you going to do about Jesus?

In other words, I avoid the fight and start moving the conversation back to Jesus. We can discuss evolution at length after they choose to follow. Or if we really want to get to the bottom of things, we can wait until we're in the heavenly kingdom and ask God about it. He's sure to have a VHS tape of the whole event that we can watch and discuss together.

The question Jesus sidestepped was about theology: The

Samaritan woman asked him whether people should worship in Jerusalem or Samaria. Jesus said that "true worshipers" must worship in spirit and truth and that the time for such things was coming.

The woman, perhaps overwhelmed by Jesus' answer, said she knew that one day the Savior of the world would come and explain this all. Then Jesus, in a moment uncharacteristic of him, said to her, "That's me. I'm the one who was sent into the world to save it."[5] (She was, by the way, the first person to whom he directly revealed himself as the Savior—a downtrodden, outcast, foreign woman.)

That's when she ran to town and shared her own good news: "Come, see a man who told me everything I ever did. Could he be the Savior of the world?"[6] Then the whole town turned out and invited Jesus to stay with them, which he did for several days, and they said, "Now we have heard for ourselves, and we know that this man really is the Savior of the world."[7]

In this story, Jesus did some things similar to what he did with Nicodemus. He

1. used an approach specific to the person with whom he was interacting,
2. used metaphor and comparison ("living water") to make spiritual truths more easily understandable,
3. tried a different approach when his communication partner wasn't getting the message clearly, and
4. started with the woman's own needs and concerns.

Notice also that he

1. took the initiative in the conversation (he started talking first) and
2. sidestepped objections to the main message he was sharing, forcing her to engage with the central message of the good news, not the arguments and concerns surrounding it.

One more note from this story: Jesus' followers didn't think the Samaritans were ready for the good news, so they didn't initiate with them. They went into town, ordered their lamb sandwiches, bought water bottles, and came back to discover Jesus talking to a woman, alone. They didn't ask him, "What are you doing talking to that woman?" or "What do you want from her?" because they were afraid of the answer.

For Jesus to present the good news in a way that was understandable to this woman required that he look bad to people around him in that moment. But Jesus' followers were the ones who were wrong, as Jesus pointed out later. The Samaritans were, indeed, "ripe for harvest."[8] Many in the town believed because Jesus initiated with an outcast woman in a town that could have been ignored and overlooked.

Don't choose for other people whether they are ready to hear the good news. I've done this myself. I hosted an "atheist Bible study" years ago, where I was slowly building to sharing the good news. One week, one of the men came in and said he would no longer be coming because he had prayed to receive Christ with a friend during the week and would now be attending a "Christian Bible study." I had thought he wasn't ready. His friend (and apparently the Holy Spirit) thought it was time. Don't put off sharing good news because you've decided whether someone will respond or not. Their response is between them and God.

There are many stories about Jesus sharing the good news about the coming Kingdom or the good news about the Savior of the world (himself!). He rarely repeated himself. During the water-drawing ceremony at the Feast of Tabernacles, Jesus announced that if any were thirsty, they could come to him and drink the living water of the Spirit, which would then flow from their hearts. The next day, no doubt standing before enormous menorahs filled with oil in front of the Temple, he told the people he is the Light of the World.

To the blind, he gave sight. To the deaf, ears to hear. To the lame, the ability to walk. To the hungry, food. He chastised the religious who were sure of themselves and comforted the brokenhearted.

Then and now, Jesus always speaks to people where they are. Many times, he waited to be asked before initiating a miracle. But he always initiated with the good news. That's a miracle he volunteered, over and over.

What do we learn from Jesus about evangelism?

1. We must see and initiate with the people around us.
2. We should speak their language and speak to their needs.
3. If they don't understand, we should try again with different words.
4. We should start with their questions and concerns, not our agenda.

This week, keep an eye open for people around you who may be open to a conversation—people who are looking for good news. Ask God for courage to speak up and to show your care for them. As believers, we are always trying to find ways to be more like Jesus. Let's pay attention this week to the way Jesus interacted with those who didn't understand the good news and try to be more like him in that.

Reflection Questions

1. In both stories in this chapter, Jesus used metaphor to make his message clear. Why do you think he used metaphor to explain spiritual things?

2. What would you need to change to do evangelism more like Jesus? Which things did he do that you find easy? Which things do you find more challenging?

3. We talked about sidestepping questions that move people away from talking about Jesus (even if they are important questions, in some sense). What topics can you imagine sidestepping? What questions are too important to sidestep?

4. Sometimes we get hung up trying to explain what behaviors of the person we're sharing with are sinful. Imagine for a moment that someone says they believe lying is a sin but covetousness is not. Both of these are in the Ten Commandments. Can someone come to Christ by repenting of their lies and not their covetousness? Do we have to repent from *all* our sins or only the ones we recognize? And if only the ones we recognize, which is more important: to find a sin they agree is evil or to convince them the obvious sins we observe in their lives (which they don't see as wicked) are evil?

Exercises

1. Jesus always did something different, depending on who he was talking to. Read the following stories of Jesus moving people toward God:

   - Luke 7:36-50 (Simon and the woman who was full of love)
   - Luke 10:25-37 (the teacher of the law)

- Luke 18:18-30 (the rich young ruler)
- Luke 19:1-10 (Zacchaeus)

Which observations from this chapter are true in these stories as well? What new observations about how Jesus does evangelism can you make from these stories?

2. Initiate a spiritual conversation with someone this week. A friend or a stranger, a family member or a coworker— it doesn't matter who, but make it a goal to start a conversation this week. (Don't wait for one! Start one.)

3. After your spiritual conversation, sit down with a pen and paper (or with a friend) for a half hour and debrief the conversation. Where did you do well in (1) seeing and initiating with others; (2) speaking to their needs, in their language; (3) trying again with different words when/if they didn't understand; and (4) starting from their questions and concerns? Where could you have done better? Pray for the seeds of the good news you have planted in their life to grow through the power of the Holy Spirit.

CHAPTER 8

THE GOSPEL ACCORDING TO BUDDHA

Finding the Good News People Already Know

"I'M THE MOST BUDDHIST PERSON I KNOW."

A college student said this to me, and I knew in my heart I had chosen the wrong person to share Jesus with.

"I'm the most Buddhist person I know," he said. "In fact, my friends and family, who are all Buddhist, always say to me, 'Hey! Could you stop being so Buddhist all the time?'"

This was one of my first times trying "random evangelism" . . . in other words, walking up to a stranger and trying to nonchalantly talk about the most deep, personal, and intimate topics imaginable, breaking all sorts of cultural taboos and making me feel like a colossal crazy person.

It was an assignment as part of my training as a missionary.

I had a whole script to use, and a tract, and here's the thing: It wasn't contextualized, not really. It was full of Christian lingo, and while it was vaguely targeted at college students, it wasn't targeted at an Asian American Buddhist college student. The message had not been translated for him.

I had used this amazing icebreaker question: "Hey, would you like to talk about spiritual things for a few minutes?" (Feel free to use that any time.)

And *it worked*. Remember, when we communicate the good news, we are participating with the Holy Spirit. We are coworkers with God. I've used so many terrible sentences to start a conversation, but God empowers them.

The student said he would love to have a spiritual conversation, and he pushed his homework aside and gave me his whole attention. Then he said, "I'm the most Buddhist person I know."

My heart sank. What I thought would be a pretty easy, "typical" conversation about Jesus became my worst nightmare: a comparative-religion argument. Best-case scenario: The guy listens politely and decides Jesus was a good teacher. Worst case: I don't know. I become Buddhist?

Instead of entering an argument, I decided to ask him what he liked so much about the Buddha. If he liked the Buddha more than even his Buddhist family, I would know he was devout and that there must be something special there.

He loved the Buddha a lot. He shared some of the beautiful ideas and teachings with me, and I listened to him for a while, just getting an appreciation of this guy and what he loved about his own religion.

Then he said, "There's just one thing that bothers me."

"What's that?" I asked.

"The Buddha said he wasn't a god, and we shouldn't worship him. But honestly, most Buddhists, that's what we do. We worship him. I wish someone would come along and say, 'I am God; you should worship me.'"

A shocked silence followed. Finally I managed to say, "Hey, I know a guy."

His eyes lit up, and he eagerly listened as I told him the story of the great teacher Jesus, who was in many ways like the Buddha, with the big, big difference being that he claimed to be God. When I reached the end of explaining the good news about Jesus, "God with us,"[1] who died and rose again so we could be in relationship with God, I asked him, "What do you think?"

He looked at me and said, "I guess I'm a Christian now."

Buddha at the Foot of the Cross

It was a strange moment as we bowed our heads together and he prayed for God's forgiveness, accepted Christ as his Savior, and became a follower of Jesus. Strange because he came into the presence of God not through the tract in my hand, not because I had a fight about Buddhism, not because of my clever arguments, but because the teachings of the Buddha brought spiritual truth that led him to the person of Jesus.

I'm not suggesting, by the way, that approaching strangers with the teachings of the Buddha is the best way to share the gospel. However, if someone is already a follower of the Buddha, it's possible the Holy Spirit, the perfect communicator, has already started using the familiar terms, ideas, thoughts, and beliefs of Buddhism to insert truths about God into someone's life. This is not to say that "all roads lead to God"—Jesus is clear that "no one comes to the Father but through me."[2] No, this is just a reminder that God is the sort of Shepherd who goes out to find his sheep. He doesn't just stand near the sheep pen and shout until his little lambs come to him.

Now, in my story, I didn't have to learn a whole lot about Buddhism or the Buddha to be able to share. My new friend was ready for a message about God because of something that bothered him about the Buddha. But I know people who do lots of evangelism among their Buddhist friends, and they would say there are great ways to share Jesus from the teachings of the Buddha.

That sounds a little crazy, I know. We're going to spend this whole chapter talking about how that might work. But before we do, let me share three quotes from the Buddha, and you think about whether you might be able to find a bridge from the words of the Buddha to the words of Jesus.

"If anyone should give you a blow with his hand,
with a stick, or with a knife, you should abandon
any desires and utter no evil words." (Majjhima
Nikaya 21:6)

"Consider others as yourself." (Dhammapada 10:1)

"If you do not tend one another, then who is there to tend you? Whoever would tend me, he should tend the sick." (Vinaya, Mahavagga 8:26.3)[3]

These aren't identical, of course, but you can certainly see some similar statements made by Jesus in Luke 6:29, Luke 6:31, and Matthew 25:45, respectively. It seems, at least, that Buddha and Jesus would have had an interesting conversation if they had been able to sit at a meal together.

But is it a good idea to do this sort of thing—start with pagan religion before getting to the good news and get to know the "other" point of view before sharing Jesus?

Evangelism with Zeus

Acts 17 gives us some good insight. It's one of my favorite stories in Scripture, and the verses I love the most are when Paul says, "From one man he made all the nations, that they should inhabit the whole earth; and he marked out their appointed times in history and the boundaries of their lands. God did this so that they would seek him and perhaps reach out for him and find him, though he is not far from any one of us."[4]

I wrote about this at length in my book *Into the Fray*, a modern exploration of the book of Acts. There's a little overlap here, but it's an important moment, and insightful for us today as we try to figure out what Paul meant when he said he became "all things to all people so that by all possible means [he] might save some."[5]

The second half of Acts 17 takes place in Athens, one of the greatest, most beautiful cities in the world at the time. It's packed with cutting-edge technology, gorgeous architecture, idols to every god imaginable, temples on every corner. Think of it as a living version of the Internet: Everyone was there, and anything you wanted was available. And there was this place called Mars Hill (or the Areopagus), where philosophers would get together and make speeches and debate and argue with one another, like a great big chat room.

Two warring religious ideas fought for dominance in the world of Greek religion and philosophy at the time: the Stoics and the Epicureans.[6] The Stoics believed God permeated everything—sort of like the Force in *Star Wars*, without the dark and light sides. God was in everything. God made up the universe. All the material of the universe—matter and energy, all of it—made up God. They would use the name Zeus to refer to God and/or the universe. They were pantheists.

The Epicureans, on the other hand, believed that Zeus and all the other gods in the Greek pantheon existed but didn't interact with human beings. The gods were so far superior they would never answer prayers or respond to human pleas any more than you or I would respond to a single bacterium crying out in distress. Reverence for the gods, religious rituals, sacrifices, and so on were less than useless, according to the Epicureans.

Paul found himself greatly distressed by the idols and religious practice of the Greeks. He wandered the city, studying their practice and their rituals. He watched their plays, learned their poetry, and saw in the midst of them all a chance to talk to the Greeks about Jesus.

Remember—Paul's *message* was the same it had always been: Jesus the Messiah, who came to save the world through his death and resurrection so humanity could be in relationship with God. Paul preached it over and over, and there are plenty of examples in Acts of him sharing this in a straightforward way, using the traditional terms and approach he often used in Jewish circles.

The *messenger* was the same. Paul was still Paul. He hadn't fundamentally changed as a human being. The *signal* was the same, too, so far as the mode of transmission: He was giving a public speech. What's different is that he *translated* the message to aid his audience as they received it, taking on the translation burden himself instead of expecting his communication partners to do it.

The way Paul did this was by knowing, understanding, and quoting from the Greeks themselves. He didn't start with Scripture; he started where the Greeks were looking for greater knowledge ("AN UNKNOWN GOD"[7]) and then pointed out places in their own theology where they had found truth about the one true God.

Paul shared the gospel by quoting first from the philosopher

Epimenides. In Epimenides's poem called "Cretica," a man named Minos corrected the Greeks who believed Zeus had died. He was a Stoic, so he didn't buy that. He said,

> *They fashioned a tomb for you, holy and high one,*
> *Cretans, always liars, evil beasts, idle bellies.*
> *But you are not dead: you live and abide forever,*
> *For in you we live and move and have our being.*[8]

So that famous quote about how we live and move and have our being in God[9] is from a Stoic poem about Zeus. In that same verse, Paul also quoted from a poem called "Phaenomena," by Aratus, telling the Greeks that their own poet said, "We are God's offspring."

> *Let us begin with Zeus, whom we mortals never leave*
> *unspoken.*
> *For every street, every market-place is full of Zeus.*
> *Even the sea and the harbour are full of this deity.*
> *Everywhere everyone is indebted to Zeus.*
> *For we are indeed his offspring . . .*[10]

One again, Paul was talking about Zeus!

The gospel of Jesus started with quoting the Stoics.

Why? Had Paul gone off the rails? Was he suggesting "all roads lead to heaven"? Was he saying Zeus and Jesus were the same person?

Not at all. He was sharing the good news in a way they

could understand: The one true God had some similarities with their understanding of Zeus. He quoted pagan poetry and philosophy to help them understand. He had read it, studied it, and memorized it. He was using their terminology, their vocabulary, and their philosophy to bring them into the conversation about Jesus.

Now, he didn't shy away from hard-to-understand topics. He made it clear that there was a big difference between Stoicism and Christianity. In fact, he dove right in to talking about Jesus and how he not only died but also came back from death.

And what was the response?

Some mocked him.

Some said they wanted to hear more.

Some believed.

Speaking someone else's language isn't a magic formula that will cause people to believe. The response may be mockery, disbelief, a desire to hear more, or confusion. But Paul wasn't afraid to use every tool at his disposal to make the good news clear, including using the religion and philosophy of his hearers to show them the way to Jesus.

We don't need to be afraid to study and get to know other religions. We don't need to shy away from using pop culture, or politics, or sports, or whatever thing might most interest our friends in the message. If talking about Harry Potter or superheroes or the latest fantasy epic or the Super Bowl or quilting or Hinduism or atheism will give us a flicker of a chance to maybe make things clearer, then let's participate with the Holy Spirit and trust that God will make the message clear if we push things too far. God can protect the message as well as translate it.

So, yes, it might be important when I talk to a Muslim to know that the Koran speaks of the "holy" Jesus who was born to his mother, Mary, who was a virgin.[11] With an atheist, I might talk about the universe coming into being with an explosion of light, or about the importance of humanity.

Jesus reveals himself in the truth of other religions not because those religions are true but because Jesus himself is the Truth, and all truth points inexorably toward him.

The Good News in Heart Languages

I love when people come to know the good news in their own language and culture. They're less likely to convert to the culture of the person who shared with them and much more likely to convert their culture toward Christ.

What I mean is, there is no reason African believers needed to start building little wooden buildings with steeples and white picket fences in the twentieth century. There is no reason they couldn't have come to Christ and learned to follow him without adopting the culture of those who brought Christ to them. The places where Christ rises up within a culture are more effective for the spread of the Kingdom and more faithful to the future vision of the Kingdom, when people from every tribe, tongue, and nation will worship God together.

Paul believed that, too, and for years a large part of his ministry was explaining that you don't have to be a Jew to follow Jesus. You don't have to be an American, or in a democracy, or a Westerner, or an English speaker to follow Jesus, either. (You also *can* be any of those things!)

One of the most beautiful things about people from various backgrounds coming to know Jesus is watching new believers internalize the good news in their own cultural context. If I allow new followers of Jesus to express themselves in their own heart languages rather than teaching them my language and expectations, they will create expressions of the good news that are already culturally attuned to others in their culture.

I love the stories of Jesus' arrival in Hawai'i, because they are so dramatic that they sound like something from two thousand years ago, but they are recent enough that we have firsthand newspaper accounts and journal entries and stories about it.

One of the early Jesus followers in Hawai'i was a woman named Lili'uokalani, the last queen of Hawai'i. Her story is, to me, a sad one. The early missionaries to Hawai'i did some wonderful, amazing things. Their children, however, got involved in the politics and financial colonization of the islands that led to the shameful annexing and eventual theft of the Hawai'ian islands by the American government. Queen Lili'uokalani was both surprised and deeply saddened that Christian people could participate in this. Although she had been grievously wronged by some she would call brothers and sisters, and wrongfully imprisoned for political reasons, she stayed deeply committed to Jesus. She wrote a hymn while under house arrest in 1895, and it has become a song that every schoolchild in Hawai'i learns.

QUEEN'S PRAYER

'O kou aloha nô	Your loving mercy
Aia i ka lani	Is as high as Heaven
A 'o Kou 'oia 'i'o	And your truth
He hemolelo ho'i	So perfect
Ko'u noho mihi 'ana	I live in sorrow
A pa'ahao 'ia	Imprisoned
'O 'oe ku'u lama	You are my light
Kou nani ko'u ko'o	Your glory, my support
Mai nânâ 'ino'ino	Behold not with malevolence
Nâ hewa o kânaka	The sins of [humanity]
Akä e huikala	But forgive
A ma'ema'e nô	And cleanse
No laila e ka Haku	And so, o Lord
Ma lalo o kou 'êheu	Protect us beneath your wings
Kô mâkou maluhia	And let peace be our portion
A mau loa aku nô	Now and forever more
'Âmene	Amen[12]

This song, written in Hawai'ian rather than in English, continues to communicate the good news to the people of Hawai'i because it is in their words, written by their queen, and it has a uniquely Hawai'ian way of expressing the good news about God. It is her continuing witness to the people of Hawai'i.

Going back to my formerly Buddhist friend, one thing I love about this method is that we can see our participation with God in the evangelism process even more clearly. God, the transmitter of good news, had already translated the words of the Buddha into something my friend began to recognize as good news. Then I was allowed to come along and take his question ("This good news seems incompatible with what I know about Buddhism . . .") and help him see the rest of the message God was already communicating to him. It's a beautiful thing to participate in!

That's an important question for us to consider with people, no matter how far away from God they seem: What is God already communicating to them about the good news? And how can I join God in that communication?

Reflection Questions

1. Evangelistic training sometimes focuses on the uniqueness of Christianity and how to point out where it's different from other religions. What do you think

about starting with the similarities and then moving
toward the differences? What are the potential risks?
Potential benefits?

2. Is there a difference between "all roads lead to God"
   and "God will go down any road to show people the
   way to salvation"? Why or why not?

3. What is the difference between starting a conversation
   using people's interests (whether religious or not) and
   the "bait and switch" technique described by Chelsea in
   chapter 3, when she complained that Christians think
   "Jesus is boring"? Is there a balance here? If so, how do
   you keep the balance?

Exercises

1. Choose someone who has a different religious belief
   than you do (not another denomination but an actual
   other religion). Get together with them and ask, "What
   do you love about your religion?" Don't interrupt or
   tell them what you disagree with. Legitimately get to
   know them and their point of view. Don't talk about
   Jesus and Christianity unless invited to do so. If you
   are invited to talk about Jesus, start with things you
   love about Jesus that are *similar* to what they love in
   their religion.

2. Talk to a stranger about spiritual things this week.

CHAPTER 9

I'M LOSING YOU

Noise in the Signal

WHEN YOU'RE TALKING on a cell phone and you start to lose bars, noise is introduced to the signal. Your friend on the other end is still talking, but you're only catching bits and pieces. Although their message hasn't changed, and they're still doing the work of communication, you're not able to understand because the noise drowns out the signal.

Anyone who has been on a conference call has experienced the comedy of errors that occurs with noise in the signal. Someone hasn't muted their call; they're sitting by their gate at the airport, and we keep hearing announcements not to leave our bags unattended. Someone else's call keeps dropping. Another is driving in their convertible, and every time they unmute, all we hear is the wind and a distant murmuring.

Meanwhile, your doorbell rings and you're getting urgent text messages.

We're all desperately trying to understand each other, but no one can hear anyone else, because there's too much noise.

It's easy to introduce noise into the signal when we're talking to someone else. And when we're communicating something as important as the good news, we need to be aware of what we're doing that might prevent someone from hearing it.

For instance, I knew a man who never tipped his servers at restaurants. He would, instead, leave religious tracts along with the exact change for his meal. "I gave them the good news of eternal life," he would say. "What could be a better tip than that?"

There are multiple issues at play here, but one is that this gentleman's actions have introduced *noise* into the signal. The message hasn't changed—it still has all the power of the gospel (if the server should happen to read through the tract). But refusing to tip (perhaps intended to communicate that Jesus is more important than money?) is not communicating the good news.

Anything that corrupts the signal is noise—for instance, leaving a generous tip, yet the server spills leftover cola on the tract; or a printing error that leaves out the final page.

The Holy Spirit Overcomes the Noise

When we confronted my cheapskate acquaintance about how his miserly interaction corrupted the signal that carried the good news, he said, "The Word of God does not return void."

In other words, God will deal with this. He'll make the message clear. And, yes, sure, there's some person somewhere who came to Jesus despite a cheap tipper. The good news with a corrupted signal is better than no good news at all. God does what he wants. He can translate a terrible, corrupted message and make it clear if he chooses.

On the other hand, this man was using that particular verse out of context to say something Scripture does not. I was taught by well-meaning people in my faith community to do the same thing when I was growing up.

So let's take a minute and examine the context of this verse. The reference is from Isaiah 55:11. The way my acquaintance was reading it, that verse tells us that God's Word (meaning the Bible) is a magic cure-all. If you quote a Bible verse, it will work its magic on your communication partners no matter what and be understood exactly as it should be understood.

Ironically, this interpretation does not understand the verse in the way it's meant to be understood. In Isaiah 55, God is talking about making a covenant with his people. As he says in verse 3, he has made an agreement with his people. And God always does what he says. He's talking about how he keeps his promises, not saying that quoting Bible verses will always be effective in a supernatural way during evangelistic conversations.

So while I absolutely believe the Holy Spirit will gladly

pick up the slack when we communicate the good news, that particular verse isn't telling us Bible verses are magic spells and will always work if we quote them right.

Okay, Matt, but I don't treat the Bible like a spell book! Who does that? you may be thinking. And my answer would be . . . More of us than you might think, Gandalf.

The impulse emerges out of good motives. Growing up in evangelical culture, I've always been taught that my most important job as an evangelist is *keeping the gospel pure*. What this means is, without a doubt, *protecting the message*. And if our job is protecting the message, the "safest" way to share that message is through quoting Scripture. I need to make sure the gospel meets a rigorous theological test, that people are hearing it correctly.

But what this means in practice is that I am going to spend my time focused on the message, not the translation. Because I've decided that my job is primarily to protect the message, I'm going to trust the Holy Spirit to do all the translation. With this perspective, it doesn't matter if there's noise. It doesn't matter if the signal is weak. It doesn't matter if I do a terrible job translating the message or say things in a confusing way. The Holy Spirit will take the magic Bible verses and make the message clear regardless, right?

This kind of thinking leads to conclusions like "My job is to share the gospel, nothing more" or "I posted a Bible verse on social media; now it's all up to God."

But I have to wonder: If God wants us to be his coworkers,

do you think he wants us to stop working before things are finished?

He gives us the message.

He tells us to share the message.

Does he not want us to participate in translating the message and making it understandable?

If we can trust God to translate the message, can we not also trust him to keep the message pure?

Leaving a tract on a table may be sufficient for someone to come to Jesus. But what if God wants us to be more involved?

Reflection Questions

1. Have you ever had a miscommunication with someone? What was the core issue in the misunderstanding? How did you eventually come to understand each other?

2. When someone shared the good news with you, did they help with the "translation," or were you left on your own? (For instance, did they use easy-to-understand terminology? Did someone explain complicated or unfamiliar words to you? Or did you have to figure it out on your own?)

3. Can you think of a time when you saw, heard, or participated in a "gospel presentation" that left people

confused or disinterested? What was that like? Was it because of "noise" or a problem with translation? Do you think the response could have been different if that had been addressed? How?

Exercises

1. Watch for poor communication this week, whether it's from a sign, in an email, in the media, or in personal interaction. What is causing the communication not to work well? How could it be improved? How would you do it differently?

2. Tell a friend you want to practice poor communication. Have them send you texts without fixing autocorrect. Have them call you with a towel over their phone (or put you on speakerphone while driving in a convertible). Have them do their best to drive you crazy with noise in the signal. As they do this, do your best to understand and respond well to their communication. How does it make you feel? What do you learn about how others might feel when there's noise in the signal?

CHAPTER 10

WHY DIDN'T YOU SAY THAT IN THE FIRST PLACE?

Jargon, Translation, and the Good News

"I COULD NEVER FOLLOW JESUS because he wants children to suffer," a college student said to me, tears brimming in her eyes.

"Why would you possibly say that?" I asked.

"I went to a church once, and they were reading from the Bible, and Jesus said, 'Suffer little children to come unto me.'[1] If children want to come to Jesus, he'll make them suffer."

"Oh," I said. "That's from the King James Bible." I pulled out an NIV. "Try this."

She read the verse: "Jesus said, 'Let the little children come to me, and do not hinder them, for the kingdom of heaven belongs to such as these.'"[2]

She wiped the tears from her eyes. "Let the little children come? So he's saying—"

"He's saying no one should stop kids who want to be near him. He wasn't some distant power; he wanted to let the kids get in close." I explained to her that the King James, while enormously beautiful, was written around the time of Shakespeare. Sometimes they used words differently than we do today. It's still the Bible, and still God's Word, but it uses language that, for the modern reader, is archaic.

"So the problem wasn't Jesus," she said thoughtfully. "It was the translation."

Which was, yes, more or less correct. The King James is a wonderful translation, but *it wasn't a good translation for her*—not at that point in her spiritual life, anyway. She hadn't understood the message because the King James wasn't speaking her language; the unfamiliar translation had introduced noise into the signal, making it difficult for her to parse the message correctly.

Agni the Hotri

I would like to ask you to read part of a Vedic hymn. If you're somewhere you feel comfortable reading it aloud, all the better:

MANDALA I, HYMN 1.

ASHTAKA I, ADHYÂYA 1, VARGA 1–2.

1. *I magnify Agni, the Purohita, the divine ministrant of the sacrifice, the Hotri priest, the greatest bestower of treasures.*

2. *Agni, worthy to be magnified by the ancient Rishis and by the present ones—may he conduct the gods hither.*

3. *May one obtain through Agni wealth and welfare day by day, which may bring glory and high bliss of valiant offspring.*

4. *Agni, whatever sacrifice and worship thou encompassest on every side, that indeed goes to the gods.*

5. *May Agni the thoughtful Hotri, he who is true and most splendidly renowned, may the god come hither with the gods.*

6. *Whatever good thou wilt do to thy worshipper, O Agni, that (work) verily is thine, O Aṅgiras.*

7. *Thee, O Agni, we approach day by day, O (god) who shinest in the darkness; with our prayer, bringing adoration to thee—*

8. *Who art the king of all worship, the guardian of Rita, the shining one, increasing in thy own house.*

9. *Thus, O Agni, be easy of access to us, as a father is to his son. Stay with us for our happiness.*[3]

How did you feel as you read this passage?

When I ask people at evangelism trainings to read this aloud, I often get responses like "confused," "nervous," "scared," "uncertain," "worried I'd mispronounce words," "I didn't know what was going on," and "I wasn't sure what I was saying."

Did you feel any of those things?

Unless you have some significant experience with Hinduism, you probably did feel some confusion or uncertainty. That's because most religious contexts are full of jargon. You felt uncertain because the words did not clearly communicate meaning to you.

Sometimes when we share the good news with people, they feel like you did when you read that passage. We use words they don't understand or words they know but that we use differently. We use jargon and specialized terms that leave them feeling confused, inferior, or frustrated.

Denotation, Connotation, and Jargon

Three words will be helpful as we move forward: *denotation*, *connotation*, and *jargon*.

Denotation is a word's dictionary meaning. For instance, if I were to say, "My mother is a woman," the denotative meaning of the word *woman* would be something like "An adult female of the human species."

Connotation is the feeling of a word. If I were to go to my mom's house and say, "Woman, please get me a sandwich!" she would not be pleased. Why? Because although the words are accurate, the word *woman* feels disrespectful in this sentence, said in this way.[4] If I responded to her displeasure by saying, "Are you not an adult female of the human species?" I promise you I would not receive a sandwich in return.

Connotation can be different for different people, families, regions, and cultures who all speak the same language. I once wrote a coworker an email and called him "buddy," which he took to be demeaning. I was thinking of the denotation ("a friend"). For me, the word had a positive connotation that held some feeling of affection. He, on the other hand, called his son "buddy" and felt that for me to call him that was to take an inappropriate top-down role in our relationship. Fortunately for me, he was kind enough to let me know how my words made him feel, and we were able to make amends (and I never called him "buddy" again).

We also need to consider jargon. *Jargon* is a word that has a different connotative or denotative meaning inside a group than it has outside a group (slang can also fall into this category).

Let's use the word *Lord* as an example. This is a great word that has a clear, specific meaning for us in the Christian community. Most of us use the word every time we pray. For instance, it's common in evangelistic presentations to say something like, "Would you like to ask Jesus into your heart as Lord and Savior?"

That phrase and the word *Lord* in this context is Christian jargon (the word *Lord* means something different for Christians than for those outside our community).

The easiest way to recognize Christian jargon is to consider how the word is used in secular settings. Ask yourself, *When do I hear the word* lord *outside church?*

Here are a few instances I can come up with:

- landlord
- warlord

- drug lord
- Lord Voldemort
- Lord Vader
- Lord of the Dance

Now, with the possible exception of Lord of the Dance, I would suggest that most of these words have a negative *connotation*. Maybe you like your landlord, maybe not. Drug lords are frightening and terrible. Vader and Voldemort are evil, controlling despots.

The *denotation* (dictionary meaning) for each word is probably still about right: someone who is in charge. But their *connotations* (the words' emotional feelings) evoke images of controlling, evil, possibly violent persons.[5]

Now, imagine again that you are sitting down with someone and asking if they want "Lord Jesus" in their life. Do you think there's a possibility they might misunderstand what that means, or that they might feel strange about it? For some, to ask if they want "Jesus as Lord"[6] might sound like you're asking them to turn their life over to a controlling, possibly evil, master.

If we're going to participate with the Holy Spirit in translating the beautiful message of the good news, this is something we'll want to pay attention to as we share. What do these words mean to the one who hears them? How do these words make them feel? Are they understanding our message correctly?

But Sin Is in the Bible

When it comes to the gospel, most of us translate naturally. For instance, the word *sin* is one we usually know we need to help out with. I might tell someone, "All have sinned and fallen short of the glory of God." Then I would explain it to them like this: "God is perfect, but we're not. We've all done wrong things." Maybe I would explain that in English, the word *sin* is most likely from Latin and means, roughly, "guilty."

When I lived in East Asia, the word for *sin* meant "crime." In other words, there wasn't an exact word for sin. So when I read the verse, "All have sinned and fall short of the glory of God,"[7] it literally said (in that language), "All have committed crimes." Oftentimes people would say, "I've never committed a crime." Then I would ask, "Have you ever done something wrong—something that broke your own moral code?" They would answer, "Of course! Everyone has!"

In this example, what I am doing is speaking to people in jargon ("sin" or "crime") and then explaining the jargon to them ("Here's what I mean when I say 'sin' or 'crime'"). I am, in other words, being careful to keep the message pure first and foremost and then explaining the jargon—which is (don't get me wrong) perfectly fine.

But what if I start without the jargon and introduce them to that later, after they join a Christian community? Do I have to use the word *sin*, or can I use words that *mean sin* instead?

Perhaps you're thinking, *I'll stick with what's in the Bible. The Bible says* sin *so I'm going to say* sin *also.*

That's a fair response.

It's also an argument similar to one people made for hundreds of years: The Bible should not be translated into the "common tongue"; instead, if people want to understand what God has to say, they should either talk to their priest or learn to read biblical Greek and Hebrew. "If we translate it," the argument went, "we will inevitably lose some of the meaning."

Now, I should also point out that *sin* is an archaic English word. It's not Greek, which means, technically, it's not "in the Bible." Although we use it in modern English translations, it's a *translated* word, not the word from the original text.

The translator's job is to take the word from the Greek (New Testament) and Hebrew (Old Testament) and compare it to the available words in the target language (in our example, English). Each word is studied for its denotative and connotative meanings, and the closest, best word is chosen.

In Greek, the word for "sin" is *hamartia* (ἁμαρτία). This word may have originally meant to be in error or to miss the mark (and originally could have been a term used in spear throwing), but it was ultimately used as a term in Greek tragedy to refer to the tragic hero's basic moral flaw or mistake (scholars are still fighting over the semantic range of this word).[8] In Hebrew, it's an archery term, *chata'* (חָטָא), which could literally mean to "miss the target's center" (it's used this way in Judges 20:16).[9] That is, you'd have hit the target but "erred" in missing the center.

That's the denotative meaning in Greek and Hebrew. Now, we can make some guesses about connotative meaning as well from using context and other places the word appears. In Old English, there were some people who took the information they had about Hebrew and Greek (and Latin—not all translations started in the original languages), and they decided on an Old English word to translate *harmartia* and *chata'*: the word *sin*.

Sin came into English from the Latin, from a root word that meant "guilt."[10] So the first people to read the English translation would have heard something close to "All are guilty, and have fallen short of the glory of God."

It's not a terrible translation, or at least it wasn't at the time. It's not perfect, either. Did *hamartia* or *chata'* carry implications (either connotative or denotative) of "guilt"? Not quite, though the idea is elsewhere in Scripture.

So when we're deciding whether we're theologically obligated to use the word *sin* when explaining the good news, remember this: *Sin* is an English word, chosen centuries ago by those trying to translate words from other languages.

Is that the best translation for the person you're talking to today? Or does the connotation or denotation give them a different, unintended meaning?

Is *sin* clearer than *wrongdoing*? Is *wrongdoing* clearer than *crime*? Is it okay to say something like "We've all messed up and fallen short of God's glory"? Or what if we just said, "We've all missed God's mark"? Is that the same as saying "sin"?

Jargon, Jargon, Everywhere

Of course, *sin* is just one word.

Imagine you and I were to meet a woman in her twenties who grew up in an atheist household. She's never talked about religion at all and doesn't know even simple Bible stories. She's never heard, for instance, the Christmas story, outside of maybe having seen the *Charlie Brown Christmas* special.

She's curious, though, and she asks us to explain what Christianity is and why it would be important for her to become a Christian.

You look at me, the guy who wrote an evangelism book, and you tell me to answer the question. So I say, "The important thing to understand is that Jesus Christ died and was resurrected as a propitiation for your sins, to the glory of God, and—though he was sinless—became sin so you might be redeemed and inherit life everlasting."

All she hears is something like *Agni the Purohita, the divine Hotri priest, and it came from a Veda*, and she is left confused and uncertain, like a kindergartner who just walked into a calculus class.

She has a bunch of questions. She's curious enough that instead of brushing those questions aside, she starts to ask them:

"Is 'Christ' Jesus' last name?"

"Redeem me? Like a coupon?"

"*Inherit* life? Wait, what? Like, he died and so I get his house or something?"

Sin? She knows that word at least. "That's stuff Christians say is wrong. Not necessarily actually wrong, like killing someone, just stuff Christians are uptight about. Church people stuff. So like, don't skip church, don't drink beer or play cards or wear a bikini—that kind of stuff, right?"

It takes about an hour to unpack that one sentence I started with, and you finally get it all explained so the young woman seems to understand. It's getting late and she has to leave. She still has questions (mostly because we used even more jargon explaining that first sentence), but she thinks she understands a little bit.

"So let me get this straight," she says. "What you meant to say is everyone messes up. Jesus never did, though. And he died and came back to life so messed-up people like me could be with God?"

"That's pretty close," you say.

She looks at you the way your teacher looked at you in high school when you did something particularly baffling. "Why didn't you say that in the first place?"

It's a question worth considering. What if we had started with "Jesus died and came back to life so messed-up people could be with God"? Who knows how far our conversation would have gone if we hadn't spent an hour explaining our jargon to her? If we had chosen to speak her language instead of the language of pews and pulpits, this young woman might have been able to learn even more about the God who loves her and wants to be in deeper relationship with her.

But then she's gone, on her way to work, and we're

standing there together, uncertain if we'll see her again. And we bow our heads and pray together that the Holy Spirit will make God's message clear to her.

Reflection Questions

1. How did you feel when reading the verses about Agni the Hotri?

2. Take a look at a gospel presentation online. Make a list of any jargon you see. How could the same message be communicated without the jargon? (If you can't find a gospel presentation, try searching for either "Knowing God Personally" or "The Bridge to Life.")

3. At some point, most followers of Jesus will have to learn jargon to interact in the Christian community. When is the appropriate time to start? What is the best way to teach such things? Should this be expected of guests at our churches or people outside the community of faith?

Exercises

1. Write a complete "gospel presentation" with no jargon at all. Or if you'd rather, rewrite someone else's gospel presentation to remove jargon.

2. Remember your friend who helped you translate something from the Bible in chapter 6? Ask them to help you with another project. Tell them you are trying to find places where you use religious jargon. Have them sit near you with a bell or buzzer from a board game. Ask them to "buzz" you every time you say a word they think might be jargon while you talk about Jesus and present the gospel. (I know this sounds like a big ask, but believe me . . . your friends will *love* using the buzzer on you. It's fun, they hear the gospel, and you get to practice saying it in their language.) Have your friend say it in their own words if you're having a hard time not using jargon.

3. Go somewhere unfamiliar and outside your comfort zone. Don't take a "guide" to explain things to you; just try to figure out the culture, jargon, and practices by yourself. This could be a place like a beauty parlor or an occasion like a comic book convention, a dog show, an unfamiliar sporting event, or a party with people from a culture different from yours. Bonus points if it's in a religious context: a Muslim gathering, a synagogue, or an unfamiliar Christian denomination.

   Pay attention to how you feel when unfamiliar things are happening around you. Does anyone offer to help explain things? Is it obvious to others that you don't know what's going on or what's being said? What percentage of what's happening do you understand?

What are the chances you're misunderstanding something? What does this say about outsiders coming into your community of faith, and how can you help people in that situation?

CHAPTER 11

MIXED SIGNALS

The Good News in Word and Deed

WHEN I WAS IN COLLEGE, this guy we'll call Brother Theo would show up and preach by the bell tower once a year. He had a stern wife and a couple of kids with big eyes. He shouted a lot about the GOSPEL and REPENT and HELL. He especially liked to scream about sex. He shouted "Fornicators!" a lot. Honestly, the students liked it when Brother Theo showed up. He brought some variety to the school year. They liked to form a circle around him and throw pennies at him while he preached, as if he were a wishing fountain. Even the kindest students found themselves searching their pockets for change.

Brother Theo liked to use the students as object lessons. He particularly liked to point out women wearing shorts and call them the "whores of Babylon." I went to school in California, where shorts-clad women are a common sight, so this formed a large part of his sermons.

Some things he said are not publishable, but his basic message was this: "You are unspeakably evil, and you are going to burn in hell." Every year he'd make some poor kid cry (nearly always a woman) by shouting at her about her clothes, makeup, and appearance. At some point, a kid in the crowd would be picked on for being "homosexual" (and if the kid protested, Brother Theo would explain that whatever sins the kid was currently involved in would lead to "becoming homosexual").

He only quoted the King James Bible, and his message was sometimes incomprehensible. It was full of jargon. One year, I remember getting in a conversation with him (which was more like shouting to each other through a crowd) where I asked, "Don't you think more people would learn about Jesus if you did this a different way? If you showed some love? If you engaged in actual conversation and not just shouting?" He looked right at me and basically said that the Bible verses would counteract any negative effects of his yelling at people.

So just to review: Here was a guy shouting at college students and calling them names and occasionally quoting Bible verses in the King James version. When asked if he thought it might be more effective to, I don't know, use the *New King James* at least, his answer was, "The Bible verses by themselves are effective, and none of those other things will get in the way."

We've already discussed this at length, but it's interesting to note that his excuse for demeaning and humiliating people was, "You should ignore all the shouting and insults—the Bible will make itself clear."

Message and Antimessage

Two messages are being sent via two different signals. On the one hand, Brother Theo is saying, "You can live with God forever in heaven" (and he did say that!), and on the other, he's saying, "You are a horrible, evil person." There may be a way to reconcile those two messages, but Brother Theo wasn't making the connections.

In the midst of conflicting messages, the people receiving the messages become confused. "Do you mean what you are saying? Are you making a joke? Are you lying or dishonest?" The typical conclusion is to believe *whichever signal is strongest*.

For instance, imagine you ask a friend to take you to the airport at two in the morning. He says, "I'd be glad to," but he's scowling, his arms are crossed, and he rolls his eyes. Then he stops talking to you for the rest of the evening.

Even if he showed up the next morning, you wouldn't expect him to be *glad*, because he had communicated one thing with his words and something else with his body language and actions.

It could go the other way too: You probably know the "lovable grump" who always says he hates people, but you don't believe him because he keeps showing up and mowing your lawn when we're sick, fixing your car, and returning your lost puppy. "Keep your stupid puppy out of my yard," he says, but the puppy won't stop licking him. It's a moment when actions speak louder than words.

Preach the Good News at All Times . . .

Whenever we start talking about words versus actions in the "evangelism" conversation, someone mentions St. Francis. They'll quote him as saying, "Preach the gospel at all times. If necessary, use words." At its best, it's a quote designed to remind us the good news is not preached in our words alone. At its worst, it's a quote people hide behind so they don't have to share the good news.

St. Francis never said it, either.[1]

Even if he had said it, his actions told a different story. I love the story about Francis where he and his friends were traveling, and St. Francis looked out and saw a field full of birds. He told his friends to wait for him, because he wanted to preach the good news to his "sisters the birds." He walked out into the field and began to preach to the birds, and according to the story, more came down from the trees to be near him and hear his preaching.[2] It appears Francis thought "using words" was often necessary.

But this popular (misattributed) quote brings up a common fight in some Christian circles. Some people believe this is an either–or thing. Either you share the good news with words, or you share good news by your actions. If you help build houses in an impoverished community, you're probably not going to share the gospel. If you go door-to-door telling people about Jesus, you're probably not going to be involved at the local homeless shelter.

"You can't preach the gospel with deeds," some will say. (You can find plenty of articles saying just that online.) This will be followed with an argument like "Imagine trying to teach someone George Washington was the first president of the United States using only body language and no words! Impossible! In the same way, it's impossible to teach even the most basic presentation of the good news using one's actions."

They're not wrong, but they're not quite right, either. You can't preach the good news with deeds *alone*.

On the other hand, you can't preach the good news with *words* alone, either. If you teach someone "God loves you—and the whole world—so much he sent his only Son so that whoever believes in him can live forever," but your actions undermine those same words because they don't show love or concern, is that really the gospel?

Also, to speak is an act. The proclamation of the good news is an act in and of itself.[3]

You can't preach the good news *by deeds alone*.

You can't preach the good news *by words alone*.

If these two modes of communication are in conflict, they

create confusion. If you try to use one without complementing it with the other, your message is incomplete. But using them together creates a harmony of meaning that boosts the individual signals.

The good news is only complete when preached in both word and deed. You can't say Jesus will bring justice and not care about justice in the world around you. You can't say that in the coming Kingdom there will be no hunger and not care that there are the hungry among us now. You can't say God loves the world and then hate your neighbor.

So yes, as we're trying to share the good news with those around us, we need to make sure we're not sending conflicting messages. We must share good words and do good deeds. We must care for people not only in our words but also in our actions. When we fail to share the good news in our words *or* our deeds, it either creates confused communication or introduces noise into the signal. But as I've found out, the good news becomes a lot clearer when actions and words work together.

One hot summer day, we had a party in our backyard. Someone knocked on the front door, and I opened it to find two sweaty young people who wanted to share with me the good news of the vacuum cleaner they were selling.

The two were a man and a woman whom we will call Steinbeck and Flannery, because I am in charge of the names around here, and my wife wouldn't allow me to name my kids either of those. Flannery was the verbose one. I told them in the first couple minutes that I wouldn't be buying anything. They begged me to let them "just clean a room" to show how it worked. (Note: Do not say yes to this.)

It was so hot, and they looked bone weary. I asked them about their work, and as is the case with many of these less-than-reputable sales companies, it turned out the poor kids only make money on commission. They get up early and are dropped off without cars in a neighborhood. No one comes to pick them up for lunch (they only get pickups if they make a sale or convince you to let them vacuum a room). Most days, they said, they work from 8:00 a.m. until 10:00 or 11:00 p.m.

I got them each a glass of water and invited them into the house. My wife and our guests kept looking in from the back porch with that familiar "What has Matt gotten himself into this time?" look on their faces.

Flannery, Steinbeck, and I were chatting now about a lot of things, and Flannery started telling me about how much she loved yoga and wanted spiritual balance in her life. I explained to her that one of my favorite things was talking with people about spiritual balance.

"Would you like to talk more about it?"

She said yes, and while we kept talking, I scooped up two plates of homemade enchiladas (we make the sauce from scratch, and I cannot exaggerate its tastiness). She and Steinbeck ate, and I talked about how Jesus had brought balance for me—how he was the center point of family, work, writing, and life, and how that made balance possible.

Then Flannery showed me her favorite tattoo (it was

of the Hindu god Ganesh) and explained how he was a remover of obstacles and a patron of arts and science. He was a god of wisdom. She said this conversation reminded her of Ganesh.

Steinbeck said that was all well and good, but he wanted to talk about how weird it was that I would let them into the house and give them something to eat and drink (where I live in the Northwest, this isn't the cultural norm).

At the end of our conversation, I wrote my phone number in some of my books, gave them to Flannery and Steinbeck, and said, "Call me if you get stranded somewhere . . . if you don't have a meal . . . if you're being taken advantage of. If you call, I will come."

They were very moved by this and asked if this was part of the balance—part of what Jesus brought into my life. I told them it was and that he is a God who would come if they called for him when they were in trouble. He is a God who cares about empty stomachs and thirsty people.

Flannery asked me if I would be willing to come to a group she met with: women in the area who led yoga classes. She wanted to know if I would come and do a presentation about finding spiritual balance. Of course, I said I would be delighted.

Steinbeck and Flannery had knocked on the doors of other Christians' homes. In fact, some had "tried to convert" them (as Flannery said). But no one had offered them a meal. No one had asked them about their day and what it was like to trudge through the summer heat selling vacuums. The simple provision of a meal and the genuine offer of hospitality had boosted the signal of the good news.

If I had only shared words with them, standing out on my front porch, they wouldn't have heard the good news as clearly. After all, they had heard the words before. If I had invited them in for a meal and offered hospitality without mentioning Jesus, they would have experienced but not understood the good news. Words and deeds together complemented and strengthened the good news so much that when Flannery and Steinbeck turned away from my house, stepping out into the neighborhood, I heard Steinbeck say, "That was amazing. What just happened?" Flannery turned and waved before they moved on to the last house, a smile on her face.

The Bible says, "Whatever you do, whether in word or deed, do it all in the name of the Lord Jesus, giving thanks to God the Father through him."[4] Let's share the good news not only in our words but also in our actions. Not only with our hands but also with our voices—so that people like Steinbeck and Flannery can hear and understand the beautiful news of the coming Kingdom of Jesus, the Savior of the world.

Reflection Questions

1. Do you prefer to share the good news with words or in your actions? Which way do you lean?

2. What do you think of the idea that we can't share good news with only good words or good deeds? Do you believe it's necessary for these things to be working in tandem?

3. What would you say to Brother Theo if you could have a quiet conversation with him away from the crowd?

4. Think of a time you were unclear about what someone was trying to say to you—when they seemed to be giving you messages that were in conflict. How did you discern which message was the "real" one? How did you decide what to believe?

Exercises

1. If you prefer to share the good news with your words, find a way to share it in your actions this week. If you prefer to share the good news through your actions, experiment with using your words this week.

2. Think back to a time when someone shared the good news with you through their words or deeds. If possible, reach out to them and tell them thank you (in your words or deeds!).

3. The next time someone shares a deep need in their life, find a way to share good news both in your active response and your verbal response.

4. Every time you see a tattoo this week, ask the person, "Why is that significant to you?" It's one of the greatest entrances to deep conversation that I know of.

CHAPTER 12

HATERS GONNA HATE

When the Good News Meets Resistance

"I HATE CHRISTIANS," Shannon said, her hands trembling and her teeth clenched. I had mentioned going to church in a casual conversation, and this was how she responded. Her anger caught me off guard. I wasn't actively trying to share the good news; I was just talking about my life, and my throwaway comment had struck a deep, throbbing wound in Shannon.

Living near Portland, Oregon, I run into people with strong, negative feelings about church often enough. Sometimes I politely ignore open hostility—it's easier to find another way and another time to discuss these things. However, Shannon had just moved into my neighborhood, and I didn't want to respond to her that way. I wanted to tell her about Jesus. But how?

You've probably had similar experiences. Maybe a neighbor sneers when you get in the car on Sunday mornings, or a coworker can't stand the Bible verse on your wall at work. Perhaps a family member or an old friend says you no longer have anything in common since you met Jesus.

Whatever the situation, it can be tough interacting with people who have emotion invested in disliking Christians. The fact is you'll still come across people who are so hurt, so angry, or so frightened that even though you try every single thing suggested in this book, they won't be able to talk about spiritual things. They'll fight even the kindest, most well-intentioned overtures to spiritual conversation.

As I thought about what to say to Shannon, I came across Proverbs 15:1: "A gentle answer turns away wrath." I wondered, *Is there a way I can use gentle words with Shannon to disarm her anger and turn her toward Christ?* Proverbs are wise sayings, not guarantees or magic formulas, so it was possible I could respond gently and Shannon might still explode in anger. But Proverbs gave me confidence that speaking with kindness might be a way forward. And it seemed like even a contextualized, heavily personalized communication of the good news at this point might be shot down and could possibly damage our relationship. She knew I was a church person and had trusted me enough to tell me she hated Christians. So there was an open door—a small, barely cracked-open door, probably with the chain still on.

I have something I try with people like Shannon. It's a simple sentence. I just say, "Tell me more about that." I've had a lot of funny conversations using those five words.

- **Me:** Hey, I'm doing a short survey about spiritual—
- *Them:* No! I hate Jesus! I hate Bible thumpers. I won't do your dumb survey.
- **Me:** Tell me more about that.
- *Them:* Christians are the worst! They are hateful and stupid.
- **Me:** Tell me more about that.
- *Them:* Well, when I was ten, this Christian kid on my block said something really mean: He said I was going to hell.
- **Me:** Tell me more about that.

I've had people tell me they don't want to talk about spiritual things and then ended up in conversations with them that lasted hours—just by saying "Tell me more about that" while they vented. It's a great way to hear and care for people, letting them talk and letting them control where the conversation is headed.

But I felt like Shannon might need something else . . . something better. So I came up with five interrelated questions I could ask Shannon and others like her.

Tell Me More

I've discussed these questions with people from many backgrounds and religious beliefs, with strangers as well as friends, with college students and coworkers, with men, with women, and even in small groups. Sometimes I talk through all five during one conversation. Other times I spread them over a series of interactions. I want to share them with you because I've found them to be "gentle answers" that turn aside people's anger about Christians well enough that they often become interested in knowing more about our loving Christ. They're a way to remove the noise from the signal for people who hate Christians or the church because of their past experiences.

1. What would you say is the worst thing Christians have done?

A simple comment about our church helping to paint a neighborhood school could make Shannon wince. "Shannon, I can see you're upset," I said the next time that happened. Then I asked my first question: "What would you say is the worst thing Christians have done in the last two thousand years?"

"The Crusades," she answered without a moment's thought, though I could tell she was surprised by my question. "Christians killing Muslims to take over Jerusalem."

Shannon's response is typical. I've asked lots of non-believing friends to identify the greatest black mark in Christian history, and most say the Crusades or the Spanish Inquisition. Other common replies (in the United States) include the Salem witch trials, the violation of Native American culture by missionaries, and slavery.

My first instinct in these situations is to defend Christianity. Some of the answers people give reflect skewed or simplistic understandings of history, and it's tempting to correct them. For instance, when my friend Jennifer talked about the hundreds of women killed in the Salem witch trials, I wanted to explain that twenty-four people died in the trials, and not all of them were women. But showing her she was wrong and I was right wasn't the point: I was trying to get past her hostility to a place where I could share the good news in her language. Remember, we're not trying to win arguments; we're trying to get a clear, well-translated message through to our friends.

So instead, I said to Shannon, "I agree. Killing innocent people is a terrible crime." This is true. No matter how many (or few) people were unjustly killed in the name of Christ, it was a horrific event. "As a follower of Jesus," I continued, "I'm also troubled by what happened in Salem."

A comment like this can take my friends off guard. I don't misrepresent my true feelings or opinions. I can agree the wrongs of the past are terrible, whether or not I share that particular interpretation of history. Taking this approach allows me to acknowledge an injustice without becoming entangled in an argument about Christianity's role in it or acting as if I myself stand accused. (And since they're sharing honestly with me, it's unlikely I'm included in the "evil Christian" category in their minds.)

When my friends see they can trust me to recognize an injustice and express compassion, they're more likely to respond honestly to what I ask next.

2. What is the worst thing a Christian has done to you?

This second question is the hardest, as the answers can be painful to hear. But it's important because it often uncovers deep hurts that are causing people's greatest anger. And so I asked Shannon, "What is the worst thing a Christian has done to you personally?"

I cried when she told me her story.

When she was a young woman, her parents forced her to get an abortion. Her favorite uncle heard what she'd done and told her, "I can't talk to you anymore. I'm a Christian, and Christians don't have anything to do with abortion." Fifteen years later, he still refused to speak to her.

Other friends' experiences aren't any better. Steven had a brick thrown through his window because he's gay. A list of Bible verses was rubber-banded to the brick so he could "see what God has to say about homosexuality." Allison was sexually abused by a leader at her church. Sam was mocked because he didn't do well on the church basketball team. Jennifer, a modern-day witch, had received verbal abuse from Christians at her college, while Jeff's youth group teased him mercilessly because he supported the wrong political party.

Although some people relate personal traumas like these,

others give generic answers such as "Christians are judgmental." If I'm asking strangers how they've been wronged, it's not surprising to hear stock responses. People share as much as they are comfortable sharing. That's okay. I don't pressure them to relate personal stories. Those who mention generic hurts may be considering their real wounds as the conversation continues. They may even choose to share those with me later, after our friendship has developed. People don't always wait for deeper relationship, though. Even strangers may gladly talk about hurts they've received at the hands of Christians, if only to prove that Christians are bad people.

Regardless of what my friends share, I don't defend the actions of those who harmed them. Nor do I speed past their answers. I've learned to keep eye contact and listen attentively. I avoid crossing my arms and leaning away from them, because these gestures communicate skepticism about what they're saying (body language is a communication signal too). I don't try to discover "the other side of the story" or push them on their interpretation of events. The fact is, whatever happened, my friends have been hurt by someone claiming to be a Christian. I want to enter into that hurt with them.

So I don't try to cheer them up or convince them it will all be better. I don't tell them the person who harmed them wasn't a Christian or "most Christians aren't like that." Instead, I mourn with them. Sometimes I cry with them.

Sometimes I apologize, like this: "Shannon, I'm sorry your uncle cut off relationship with you. I can only imagine how painful that must be." At times, I've apologized on behalf of Christians in general: "Steven, I'm sorry you've experienced Christians as hateful and unloving. I hope we'll do better in the future." I also make sure they know they can trust me not to repeat the wrong: "Shannon, I'll never cut off our relationship because I disagree with something you've done." (Honesty is key here—don't say it if it isn't true.)

I linger on this part of the conversation as long as my friends have more to say. People assume a lack of sincerity if I push past their experiences to a gospel presentation. Instead, I focus on being patient and showing love through my empathy (even when it's painful for me to do so).

The horrible things that have been done to them have become conflated with Jesus in their minds. They feel he's abusive or hateful or cruel because they've experienced Christians to be abusive, hateful, or cruel.

Most of them, it turns out, disagree with themselves. They don't really think Jesus is any of those things—not in the deepest part of their hearts. The third and fourth questions can help them realize this for themselves.

3. What was Jesus' main message?

Question three is the easiest: "What was Jesus' main message?" Without exception, everyone I've asked—Shannon, Jennifer, Steven, and Allison included—has said the same thing: love.

I reinforce this conclusion simply and quickly. As we

talked about in the last chapter, finding a place where we agree rather than disagree can be a wonderful way to move forward in talking about the good news.

"That's a great answer," I'll say. "Jesus told people the two most important commands in the Bible are 'Love the Lord your God' and 'Love your neighbor as yourself.'" If the person is interested, we might look at this conversation in Scripture together.[1] Or I might point out John 13:34: "A new command I give you: Love one another. As I have loved you, so you must love one another." These verses affirm Jesus' clear emphasis on love.

My friends have shown deep theological insight in their answers, and I want to acknowledge and celebrate that. I don't say things like "Yes, Jesus' message is about love, but ultimately it's about God glorifying himself." I don't even have to pull out my Bible and show them chapter and verse—I can say, "Yes, that's what Jesus said to his followers, word for word: 'Love one another.'" I don't spend much time on people's replies to this question, other than to highlight our agreement. Their response leads naturally to question four.

4. Do these actions reflect the true teaching of Jesus?

The fourth question is, "If it's true Jesus' main message was love, would you say the actions of the people from the first two questions reflected the true teachings of Jesus?" The answer is self-evident. Everyone agrees that people actively following Jesus' teachings about love will not participate in genocide, abuse people sexually, cut off relationships for imperfection, or maliciously inflict pain on those around them.

When I posed this question to Shannon, her eyes lit up. "No!" she said. She had just taken pieces of information she already had and put them together in a different order in her mind. Her old perspective said her uncle had hurt her because he was a Christian, so she concluded "Christians are bad." She now realized that, yes, her uncle had hurt her and, yes, he was a Christian, but his unloving actions weren't in line with Jesus' teachings. That led her to a new conclusion: "Although my Christian uncle has done painful things to me, Jesus is not reflected in those things." Shannon's changed perspective was especially powerful because she arrived at it on her own, not because I had "corrected" her.

This was an excellent time to ask Shannon the last question.

5. Would you like to know more?

"Shannon," I said, "would you like to know more about the actual teachings of Jesus?"

She responded with a voracious desire to do so. When someone expresses direct interest in learning more about Jesus in the Bible, they often have greater patience for learning new terms, new history lessons, jargon, and so on. Regardless, I try to minimize those things in the Scripture translation we use and the way I speak. Learning those things at a less overwhelming rate is more likely to keep someone engaged. If you're in a long-term relationship with this person (or willing to be!), it's a great time to suggest reading through one of the Gospels together, maybe taking a portion at a time and meeting once a week to discuss it. Or you could watch a movie about Jesus together. Or maybe they'll want to get together regularly to ask questions about Jesus and Christianity. Maybe they'll even want to go to church.

If I invite people to church, it's important to prepare them for what they will experience. This is part of communication too. I want to make sure that the traditions, rituals, and preferences of my church communicate correctly to my friend (rather than communicating "you don't belong here").

Many churches are targeted toward longtime believers in their communication style. The message as well as the way it's transmitted shows that. So if your friend is a complete stranger to church, they might need a cultural guide and translator: When do you stand up and sit down? Is it okay not to sing the songs? How does my church welcome visitors? What do people typically wear? What terms might be unfamiliar? Are visitors expected to give money?

I want to prepare my friend so they won't feel like an outsider. If your friends are insecure around Christians or feel unsafe, it may be better to start small, perhaps by introducing them to a trusted Christian friend over coffee. Let them make some friends before diving into the whole community.

Not everyone responds positively to the last question, "Would you like to know more about the actual teachings of Jesus?" Some people still aren't interested. That's what happened with Steven: "I get it. Some Christians do bad things, but that doesn't mean Jesus is bad. I still don't want to know more about his teaching."

It's disappointing when people connect all the dots and then don't want to look at the picture they've drawn. When that happens, I keep my responses polite but honest. "I'm sorry to hear that, Steven," I might reply, "but I understand." And I leave the door open for future conversations: "If you ever have questions, I'm available."

I also like to let people know I value how they opened up about their past. "Thanks for telling me about the brick being thrown through your window," I'd say to Steven. "That must have been terrifying, and I appreciate that you trusted me enough to share that experience." Steven's my friend, and I'm not going anywhere. But we had a great conversation, and that's something to celebrate in any friendship.

A No-Lose Situation

After hearing about these conversations, you might wonder, *Does asking these questions always go so smoothly?* No, it doesn't.

I have talked to a few people who were implacably committed to their anger, and nothing I said was going to change that. One woman translated my inquiries as "Bible thumping." I silently asked God to allow her to set aside her hostility. Our conversation improved, but her anger still flared up as we talked. There's not much to be done in a brief interaction with a person who is reacting this way. I eventually abandoned the conversation, saying, "I can see I've upset you. That wasn't my intention. I care about your opinion, and if you'd like to discuss this in the future, I hope you'll let me know."

Encounters like that are the exception, however. I find most people surprisingly open and even thankful as we walk through the questions. Sometimes the second question's emotional intensity makes it better for us to leave the conversation there, but even then, we've established a bond that allows me to pick up the dialogue later. For instance, when Sam shared about being made fun of at church, I didn't want to hurry him through processing his feelings. He wasn't ready to move on. But a couple weeks later I said, "I've been thinking about what you shared a while back. Do you think those people who made fun of you on the church basketball team were acting in a way consistent with Jesus' teachings?"

However the conversation happens, whether all at once or spread out over a month, people are coming to a clearer understanding of who Jesus is. And by the end of our dialogue, they know a Jesus follower they trust enough to share their deepest thoughts, hardest questions, and greatest criticisms about Christianity.

When faced with people hostile toward Christianity, these questions can help. Asking them takes courage, but the risk is minimal. The worst-case scenario is that my friends remain spiritually hostile. More often, I've found myself growing into deeper friendship with people who want to explore what it means to be the kind of Christian I'm trying to model: a loving, friendly one who listens. And the hope is these conversations lead to other conversations where my friends become my brothers and sisters in Christ.

Reflection Questions

1. How would you answer the five questions in this chapter?

2. Who is the person most hostile to God that you've personally known? Do you think these questions would have helped or hindered in a conversation with them?

3. Think through your church or community of faith. What things would you need to prepare your friends for if they were to come visit? How would you prep them?

Exercises

1. Reach out to someone you think of as hostile to Jesus/Christianity/the good news. Ask them, "What's the worst thing Christians have ever done?" If they

respond, try to go through the other questions with them as well.

2. Spend some time in prayer for those in your life who are hostile to God. Ask God to help you see them in the same way the Holy Spirit sees them. Is the Spirit already at work in their lives? How can you participate?

CHAPTER 13

I HAVE GOOD NEWS FOR YOU

Taking the Initiative to Be Messengers of the Good News

"I JUST TALKED TO A SATANIST," my friend said.

My ears perked up. I love talking to those who are furthest away from Jesus. Maybe it's partly that the conversation can't go too-far wrong. If they're the furthest away from Jesus they can be, what's the worst-case scenario? That they're still the furthest away they can be at the conversation's end.

We were in St. Augustine, Florida, and the Satanist in question was a man with stringy blond hair, a long jacket, and a permanent squint to his eyes. His name was Percival. I found him on the cobblestone streets and invited him to lunch.

Percival was homeless but made a decent living for himself by convincing other youths to join various made-up religions he invented. It delighted him, and he laughed uproariously as he told me he had convinced a gaggle of black-wearing "Goths" to put on all white and pour clean water into basins at midnight while chanting nonsense words of his own devising.

He was a Satanist, yes, but he enjoyed messing with other people. He had no patience for the Christian God. We had a conversation that ranged all over the place, but I did my best to stick to his terminology and way of speaking, and I could see it was sinking in. Finally at one point he said, "I've never understood why anyone would follow Jesus. But the way you explain it, I'm starting to see why someone might make that choice."

Our conversation ended in a little courtyard near an old tree. I asked him if I could pray for him, and he agreed to allow it so long as I didn't touch him or try to remove his "spirit guide." So we stood there in the heat, sweating but not touching, as I prayed the good news into his life. I gave him my phone number written on a religious tract.

He never called. I don't know what happened to him. But I do know this: I participated with the Holy Spirit to the fullest extent possible in that conversation. I worked hard to make the good news clear to this young man who was so broken, so lost, and so far from seeing the gentle love of a God who wants him to come into the family.

Into the Darkness

We've spent a lot of time in this book talking about how to have conversations about the good news. When the conversation starts, we know what to do. We share the message and participate with the Holy Spirit in trying to make the message clear. It's a beautiful honor.

As we come toward the end of this book, it's important for us to consider those in our families, workplaces, and neighborhoods who don't know Jesus. It's tempting to wait for them to come to us and bring up some terrible thing so we have an entry point to talk about Jesus.

Of course, that happens sometimes, and we're thrust into the middle of someone's life. A marriage falls apart, or a tragedy happens at work, and we're invited into conversation with people about spiritual things. When our neighbor died, my family had an entry into their home for a few days as they processed their grief and we helped them get their house in order.

But what about the people who are sitting outside in the dark while we're celebrating in the warmth and light of Christ's love? We can wait for them to come to us, and some of them will. But Jesus wants us to go into the darkness, not just wait for the people far off to approach the light.

Jesus, after all, came into the world to save it, not to condemn it. In Matthew 28:16-20, he told us to go to all the world in his authority and share the good news. He said it again in Mark, again in Luke, and again in Acts. In John, he said he's sending us in the same way he was sent.[1] And Paul and the early church saw fit to send missionaries around the world to tell others the good news.

The only time Jesus told us to "wait around" was when he

said to wait for the Holy Spirit to empower us.[2] That's excellent advice. We shouldn't be trying to do this alone, because only God can make the complexity of spiritual reality truly clear to someone.

So let's not wait for someone to come to us. Let's take the good news to our friends, our family, and the people around us.

Let's Make a Plan

If we're going to be active participants with the Holy Spirit, we shouldn't be sitting around passively waiting for something to happen. I've put together a list of six questions for you to prayerfully consider. These aren't questions to haphazardly brainstorm. Remember, we're meant to do this in community with one another and the Holy Spirit. So as you sit down to consider each question, be sure to do it in a spirit of prayer, and if you choose to do it with other believers in your family, church, or neighborhood, all the better!

1. Who in my life needs Jesus?

Spend some time praying about the people you know, whether nearby or far off. Whom do you know and care about who aren't followers of Jesus? Are there people who seem interested in spiritual things but never quite follow through? Whom does the Spirit bring to mind when you ask who needs to know God? Try to make a list of at least ten people. They can be acquaintances or close friends, family or coworkers, neighbors or social media connections. Make the list, and then look at it occasionally, reminding yourself whom you're wanting to share God's love with.

2. What are their deepest needs, concerns, and questions?

Remember how Jesus started his evangelistic conversations with the deepest needs of the people he interacted with? Knowing what someone's concerns and questions are can help us start conversations in the places that are most important to them. If there are people from your list whom you want to share with, you can start with these sorts of questions. You're about to talk about your spiritual lives, which is one of the most intimate possible topics. A good warm-up may be talking about what their needs, worries, and questions are. To communicate clearly and well requires vulnerability, and to communicate the good news requires both vulnerability and compassion. The topic of your friend's deepest needs and concerns is a good place to warm up and practice.

3. What is the best "signal" to communicate the good news to them?

So now you know the message well, and you're learning to translate it into your words. The question here is, What is the best mode to communicate with this person—is there a tool that would be helpful? Do they love movies? Maybe there's one that would help get the message across. Maybe this person will hear the good news best in community, so what's the best way to bring them into church or youth group or Bible study, or just to get them to hang out with other Christian friends? Basically, if you get a chance to choose the signal, what would be your first choice? How can you prepare yourself to be ready to go with this particular signal? What signal would be the worst?

4. How can I learn their "language" better? How do I best translate the good news?

Whether it's a Brony, a Belieber, a Hindu, a Buddhist, or an atheist, how can you better get to know them, their vocabulary, and their way of looking at the world? If you're going to be a fluent translator, you need to be fluent not only in the jargon and language of the church but also in their jargon and language. How can you do that? What do you need to read? How can you grow into an insider in their community? One note I'd share on this one: Take your time and learn the language. Fluency takes time and practice. Spend time really learning, not trying to teach.

5. Pray for opportunities to share the good news.

Ask God for specific chances to share the good news both with people on your list and with strangers or those who have not yet come to mind. Pray specifically and with time limits, like this: "God, please give me an opportunity to share the good news with Ted in the next ten days." Be expectant, watching for the opportunity. When it comes, jump on it!

6. Take the initiative to share the good news.

Taking the initiative to share the good news doesn't necessarily mean you have to run alongside a chariot and ask someone what they're reading (I mean, it could, but not necessarily). It means you are looking for opportunities to start a spiritual conversation, not just waiting for one to fall into your lap. This could be as simple as asking, "How are you doing?" or "Can I have a glass of water?" We don't easily move into good conversations about the good news without showing interest in and engaging with people. Be the sort of person who notices and engages other people. "Taking the initiative" means one simple thing: Be the first one to speak up about spiritual things. Do it appropriately and with kindness, and know this will most often make people love you more, not less. It's nice to know that people care.

Light in the Darkness

I've done a lot of evangelism trainings for college students. At some point, someone always asks, "I thought I was supposed to stay away from all the parties and sinners because I'm a Christian." In other words, "Shouldn't I stay away from all the darkness and evil in the world?" To which I always say, "The light shines brightest in the darkness."

We don't need to avoid the darkness. Those places that are the most frightening and dangerous, the most corrupt and evil, are in the greatest need of our presence. This is why Christians are beloved in many places in the world—where things were bleakest and most hopeless, someone showed up with the light of Christ.

When people see us as strangers, Bible thumpers, and

Jesus freaks, it's most often because we're failing in our role as translators. Of course we seem like foreigners when we speak some other language. Of course we seem like Bible thumpers when we enter into conversations without love. Certainly we seem like freaks when we ignore the deep needs shared with us, glossing over them so we can say the name of Jesus faster.

The end of the matter is this: If we truly love God, we'll want to tell others about him. I believe you do love him, and despite any fear or worries you may have, you honestly want to tell others about him. Likewise, if we truly love others, we'll not only want them to live the better life available in Christ but also gladly do the extra work of telling them all about it in their language.

As we reach the end of this book, I want to share a beautiful letter I received from a college student who was at a conference where I spoke. We'd been talking about taking the initiative to walk into the dark to tell others about Jesus.

I've changed her name and edited details pointing to her identity, but her message is something she wanted to share with her fellow college students:

Dear Matt,

I don't know if you will read this from up front, but thank you for asking people to go into the dark. My life has been a broken, shattered place.

My freshman year into my sophomore year I was deeply addicted to crank, heroin, and meth. I lived as a prostitute in a brothel owned by my boyfriend's best friend. I lived in darkness, surrounded by depression, rape, and addiction.

In the darkness, one man came to me one night when I was standing on a corner. He was wealthy, well dressed, and full of love for God. He spoke to me as a real woman for the first time. He told me I was loved by a Creator Savior. I didn't know what that meant, but it was my first conversation that made me take a step toward God.

I am a senior now and lead a Bible study. I am dating a godly man and going on a missions trip this summer and joining the staff of a Christian ministry after I graduate.

Love,

Rebecca

Jesus brings people to himself however he pleases. Televangelists who don't know Christ lead people to God. A Christian picks up a hitchhiker and changes his life forever by telling him the good news. A rich man walking in a bad part of town stops to tell a young prostitute she was made by a Creator Savior and is worthy of respect. And sometimes, being a messenger of the good news just takes trusting God enough to step into dark places, carrying the light.

How It All Works

I don't pretend to understand how God calls people into relationship.

Once when I was in my twenties, I was on the pier by the Santa Cruz boardwalk, barking at the sea lions. It was the middle of the night. Like I said, I was in my twenties.

There were three older people (late twenties, probably) sitting nearby, drinking out of red Solo cups. One of them called, "Hey, what are you doing?"

"I'm talking to the sea lions," I said.

"Do they understand you?" he asked.

"They're barking back, aren't they?"

"Come here," he said. "What are you doing here?" (He assumed, for some reason, that I was from out of town.)

I shrugged and said, "I'm in town for a few weeks, talking to people about spiritual things."

He seemed interested. I took a gospel tract from my pocket and started walking him through it. His friends laughed the whole time, making fun of him, but when I said, "Jesus has provided a way to God through his death and coming back to life," he started to weep and say, "That is so beautiful!"

And when I asked, "Do you want to pray and become a follower of Jesus?" he said he did, and he prayed, asking for forgiveness for all his sins and pledging his life to Christ. He told me he lived in a van and where he'd be parked the next day.

I brought him a Bible the next morning, and when I

knocked on his van door, he answered, confused, his hair in the middle of an argument about which way to go. He didn't remember me, and when I told him he had prayed to make Jesus his personal Lord and Savior the night before, he sneered and said he was so wasted the night before he didn't remember anything. He was skeptical he had ever said such a prayer.

I don't know how it all works. We hold drunk people responsible for their bad behavior, so perhaps they get credit for their good behavior. Maybe one day that guy will die and be surprised to find himself walking golden streets with the saints. "How did I get here?" he may ask. In which case, hunt me down and introduce us. I'll explain it to him.

There's so much we don't know about the mechanism of salvation. There are theologians lined up ready to argue about how atonement happens, when exactly we are chosen by God, and how exactly we choose to follow. Those are important and interesting conversations. What is more important, though, is the practical question, How am I going to be a part of that story with others? How can we become "all things to all people so that by all possible means [we] might save some"?[3]

I don't know exactly how it all works, but I do know this: God has put you right where you are for a reason.

I mentioned earlier that one of my favorite verses in Scripture is found in Acts 17:26-27, from Paul's sermon in Athens. He says, "From one man [God] made all the nations, that they should inhabit the whole earth; and he marked out their appointed times in history and the boundaries of their lands. God did this so that they would seek him and perhaps reach out for him and find him, though he is not far from any one of us."

God has chosen the exact time and place where we live for one purpose: so we would look for him, and maybe reach out and find him.

So often I tell someone the good news, and they say something like "My aunt always tells me she wishes I would hear about her Jesus." In Costa Rica, a student I shared with said, "Every night I pray, 'God, if you are real, reveal yourself to me.' I believe you are the answer to my prayers."

God has chosen to give your neighbors and coworkers, your family members and the person next to you on your commute, the maximum chance to seek him out and perhaps find him. And you and I, we have a chance to be God's coworkers! We have a chance to be an answer to their prayers.

Somewhere right now, there's a college kid slinging on a backpack and heading to class. There's a woman standing under a streetlamp. A guy ringing up groceries. A kid living on the street. Maybe it's here, or maybe it's overseas. Someone reading this book is going to cross paths with them and share the good news. Your neighbor bought the place next to you for a reason: God brought them into proximity with you. The person bagging your groceries has been put there to give them a shot at knowing Jesus. They're waiting for you. They're waiting for us.

Let's give them good news for a change!

Reflection Questions

1. What has been the best, most helpful aspect of this book for you?

2. What has been the most challenging or difficult thing?

3. With which of your friends would you most enjoy a deeper conversation about evangelism and the good news? Do you think they'd be open to reading and/or discussing the concepts in this book?

4. God has chosen the exact time and place where we live so people might reach out for God and perhaps find him. What questions does this bring up? What does this say about the people around you?

Exercises

1. Read through any one of the Gospels, remembering each story in it is, by definition, part of the "good news about Jesus." What new insights, questions, or thoughts does this provide?

2. Look back through all of the end-of-chapter exercises in this book. Do you remember one that made your hands sweat, so you decided to leave it undone? Prayerfully consider trying it this week.

3. Write out your answers to the six questions in the body of this chapter. Make a plan to take the initiative with the people around you who don't know Jesus.

4. Don't go alone. Share your "initiative plan" with one of your Christian friends, and ask them to pray and/or participate with you in it.

ACKNOWLEDGMENTS

JR FORASTEROS READ THIS BOOK FIRST, and everyone who made it this far has a lot to thank him for. He did the heavy lifting so you could enjoy this thing. As always, thank you for your insights, your feedback, and your friendship.

Sarah Atkinson told me I would love Don Pape, and she was right! Don is great! Let's all do more books together! Sarah, it might be time to brush off our Zombie Vampire Amish Romance book for Don. It is nonfiction. Set in Canada. In the twenty-second century. You will love it. I am so thankful for both of you. Your friendship and your encouragement mean a great deal to me.

Wes Yoder, I think this is our seventh book together! You are such a delight. It's an honor to be your friend. Thanks for finding homes for all these books.

Caitlyn Carlson did the developmental edits on this book, and she is amazing. Seriously. She restructured this whole thing from the mess I had given her and helped bring out the warmth, humor, and insights I had hoped would be in the first draft. Caitlyn, you are so talented, and you made this book immensely better. I loved working with you.

Cheryl Boyd also gave me early encouragement as I wrote this book. Thank you so much, Cheryl. It helped to know I was on the right track!

My parents, Pete and Maggie, have been examples of how to live the Christ-centered life for a lot of years. In addition, they're the ones who first explained the good news to me in a way that made sense. Thank you, Mom and Dad! You're amazing.

Shasta, you were the good news to me so often. You shaped my understanding of what it means to love others enough to share good news with them. The way you embraced the image of God in everyone around you was beautiful and inspiring. I miss you so much. We all do. Thank you for your love, light, and kindness.

So many other people gave help or encouragement along the way: Clay, Jen, Amanda, Greg and Charmaine, David, Jermayne, Wendy and Josh, and on and on. Many, many thanks.

Thank you to my long-suffering family, who puts up with the sound of computer keys clacking when they are just trying to sing the lyrics to *Hamilton* or practice ukulele or read *Harry Potter*. Special thanks for not complaining when part of the book had to be written on our vacation. Krista, you have been an inspiration in so many ways related to this book, and I'm thankful for your advice. Zoey, Allie, and Myca, I am so proud of each of you and the many ways you share the good news with the people in your lives. I love all of you.

Special thanks to the staff and partners of Cru, who have taught me so much about evangelism and given me a lot of space to experiment and try new things. I am thankful for you.

Lastly, to you, my dear reader, who read to the end of the acknowledgements even though it's a lot like reading the notes in someone else's yearbook. Thank you for not just reading this book but trying it out. It's an amazing thought to me that you may walk into a conversation this month where someone will come to know Jesus because you are participating with the Holy Spirit. People are waiting for you! Go tell them good news!

CONTACT PAGE

I love hearing from my readers!

Connect with me on Facebook (facebook.com/mikalatosbooks), via email (matt@capeville.net), or by writing on and launching a sky lantern. Check out my other books at www.mikalatos.com or my podcast at StoryMen.us.

NOTES

INTRODUCTION—GOOD NEWS ABOUT EVANGELISM

1. See Philippians 1:18.

CHAPTER 1—THE GOSPEL ACCORDING TO GOD: THE UNCHANGING MESSAGE OF THE GOOD NEWS

1. See John 3:17 and 1 John 4:10.
2. Romans 3:23.
3. Romans 6:23.
4. Emphasis added.
5. See Luke 24:48.

CHAPTER 3—THE GOSPEL ACCORDING TO "THEM": EVERYONE WANTS GOOD NEWS

1. See Romans 6:23.

CHAPTER 4—DISCERNING THE GOOD NEWS: THE IMPORTANCE OF LEARNING TO LISTEN

1. 1 Corinthians 3:6, author's paraphrase.

CHAPTER 5—CAN YOU HEAR ME? COMMUNICATION AND THE GOOD NEWS

1. See Romans 5:8, 1 John 4:19, and Micah 7:18, respectively.
2. See Jeremiah 1:11-16.

CHAPTER 6—THE GOSPEL ACCORDING TO TWILIGHT SPARKLE: CREATING FLUENT TRANSLATIONS OF THE GOOD NEWS

1. See Acts 3:1.
2. Acts 3:6, author's paraphrase.
3. See Acts 3:4-8.
4. I imagine there are probably some Bronies reading this. I want to make it clear that I know many Bronies are also Christians! This should be an easy exercise for you because you know Bronies well. But since this is an exercise meant to get us thinking about how to speak to someone outside our normal culture, maybe try "How would I share Christ with a Juggalo?" instead of "How would I share Christ with a Brony?"
5. 1 Corinthians 9:19-23.
6. See Isaiah 1:18 and Matthew 26:28.
7. See Galatians 2:11-13.
8. See 1 Corinthians 9:20.
9. If you don't go to church or are between churches, find a podcast or recording of a pastor or other spiritual leader you like and do the same exercise. Thought you were going to get out of this one, didn't you?

CHAPTER 7—JESUS THE EVANGELIST: WHAT IS GOOD NEWS FOR THIS PERSON?

1. See Matthew 16:23.
2. John 3:4, author's paraphrase.
3. John 3:10, author's paraphrase.
4. John 4:10, author's paraphrase.
5. John 4:26, author's paraphrase.
6. John 4:29, author's paraphrase.
7. John 4:42.
8. See John 4:35.

CHAPTER 8—THE GOSPEL ACCORDING TO BUDDHA: FINDING THE GOOD NEWS PEOPLE ALREADY KNOW

1. See Matthew 1:23.
2. John 14:6.

3. *Jesus and Buddha: The Parallel Sayings*, ed. Marcus Borg and Ray Riegert (Berkeley, CA: Ulysses Press, 1997), 17, 3, 21, respectively.

4. Acts 17:26-27.

5. 1 Corinthians 9:22.

6. Check out Acts 17:18.

7. See Acts 17:23.

8. "Epimenides," *Wikipedia*, accessed January 8, 2018, https://en.wikipedia .org/wiki/Epimenides#Cretica. This English translation of Epimenedes's "Cretica" is by Prof. J. Rendel Harris, who shared his edited, translated version in the following issues of the *Expositor*: October 1906, April 1907, and April 1912.

9. See Acts 17:28.

10. Dr. Riemer Faber, "The Apostle and the Poet: Paul and Aratus," *Clarion* 42, no. 13 (1993), accessed at http://spindleworks.com/library/rfaber/aratus.htm.

11. It really does! Check out sura 19:19-21 of the Koran at http://www.islam101 .com/quran/yusufAli/QURAN/19.htm.

12. "Queen's Prayer (Ke Aloha O Ka Haku) - by Queen Lili`uokalani," Huapala, accessed January 8, 2018, http://www.huapala.org/Q/Queens_Prayer.html.

CHAPTER 10—WHY DIDN'T YOU SAY THAT IN THE FIRST PLACE? JARGON, TRANSLATION, AND THE GOOD NEWS

1. Matthew 19:14, KJV, author's paraphrase.

2. Matthew 19:14.

3. *The Sacred Books of the East*, ed. Max Muller, vol. 46, *Vedic Hymns, Part II*, trans. Hermann Oldenberg (Oxford: Clarendon Press, 1897), 1.

4. By the way, this is why it seems so weird when Jesus says to the Samaritan woman at the well, "Woman, . . . believe me, a time is coming when you will worship the Father neither on this mountain nor in Jerusalem" (John 4:21). In Aramaic, this wouldn't have been disrespectful, but translated literally into English, it sounds rude. Imagine it more as Jesus saying, "Miss, a time is coming . . ." and the connotative meaning of the word comes across more clearly (although the denotative meaning has been altered).

5. And for English speakers, the connotations would be different for, say, British and American English speakers. There are more familiar, positive usages of *lord* in British culture. Then there's the House of Lords, not to mention Lord and Lady Grantham and others. So an American *Star*

Wars fan and a British *Downton Abbey* fan might have wildly different connotative responses to the word.

6. We've lost most of the original connotative (and denotative) meaning that made *Lord* a good translation once upon a time. In Middle English, the word is *hlāfweard*, which means, roughly, "loaf warden." That's *loaf*, like a loaf of bread, and *warden*, like *protector*. In medieval times, a "lord" was one who lived in the castle. The serfs were farmers and servants who worked the land. The land didn't belong to them (not much did). All the crops belonged to the lord. The lord's job was to make sure all his people were cared for. If one field failed, everyone would still be fed by the lord. If raiders came, everyone would retreat inside the castle, and the lord would protect them. For those with a good lord, he was both protector and provider. So the original connotation would have been *someone to whom I give everything and who provides all my needs and keeps me safe from harm.* That was a pretty good translation choice!

7. Romans 3:23.

8. For a short but insightful comparison of the classical origins versus the New Testament use of *hamartia*, check out William Barclay's *New Testament Words* (Louisville, KY: Westminster John Knox Press, 2000), 118–25. Or just take my word for it, but I went to all this trouble to make an endnote and everything.

9. *Blue Letter Bible*, s.v. "Strong's H2398—chata'," accessed August 23, 2016, http://www.blbclassic.org/lang/lexicon/lexicon.cfm?Strongs=H2398&t=KJV.

10. *Oxford Living Dictionary*, s.v. "sin," accessed August 23, 2017, https://en .oxforddictionaries.com/definition/sin.

CHAPTER 11—MIXED SIGNALS: THE GOOD NEWS IN WORD AND DEED

1. Glenn Stanton, "FactChecker: Misquoting Francis of Assisi," The Gospel Coalition, July 10, 2012, https://www.thegospelcoalition.org/article /factchecker-misquoting-francis-of-assisi/.

2. *The Little Flowers of St. Francis of Assisi* (Start Publishing, 2012), chapter XVI, https://books.google.com/books?id=dvjsAgAAQBAJ&printsec=frontcover &dq=little+flowers+of+st+francis&hl=en&sa=X&ved=0ahUKEwj2qKSNw LXZAhUPx2MKHTsNC8gQ6AEIKTAA#v=snippet&q=my%20little%20 sisters%20the%20birds&f=false.

3. If you don't mind losing an entire weekend, plug the words *speech act theory* into your search engine. Soon you shall be performing locutionary acts with all the best philosophy majors.

4. Colossians 3:17.

CHAPTER 12—HATERS GONNA HATE: WHEN THE GOOD NEWS MEETS RESISTANCE

1. See Mark 12:29-31.

CHAPTER 13—I HAVE GOOD NEWS FOR YOU: TAKING THE INITIATIVE TO BE MESSENGERS OF THE GOOD NEWS

1. See John 20:21.

2. See Luke 24:49.

3. 1 Corinthians 9:22.

THE NAVIGATORS® STORY

T HANK YOU for picking up this NavPress book! I hope it has been a blessing to you.

NavPress is a ministry of The Navigators. The Navigators began in the 1930s when a young California lumberyard worker named Dawson Trotman was impacted by basic discipleship principles and felt called to teach those principles to others. He saw this mission as an echo of 2 Timothy 2:2: "And the things you have heard me say in the presence of many witnesses entrust to reliable people who will also be qualified to teach others" (NIV).

In 1933, Trotman and his friends began discipling members of the US Navy. By the end of World War II, thousands of men on ships and bases around the world were learning the principles of spiritual multiplication by the person-to-person teaching of God's Word.

After World War II, The Navigators expanded its ministry to include college campuses; local churches; the Glen Eyrie Conference Center and Eagle Lake Camps in Colorado Springs, Colorado; and neighborhood and citywide initiatives across the country and around the world.

Today, with more than 2,600 US staff members—and local ministries in more than 100 countries—The Navigators continue the process of making disciples who make more disciples, advancing the Kingdom of God in a world that desperately needs the hope and salvation of Jesus Christ and the encouragement to grow deeper in relationship with Him.

NAVPRESS was created in 1975 to advance the calling of The Navigators by bringing biblically rooted and culturally relevant products to people who want to know and love Christ more deeply. In January 2014, NavPress entered into an alliance with Tyndale House Publishers to strengthen and better position our rich content for the future. Through *The Message* Bible and other resources, NavPress seeks to bring positive spiritual movement to people's lives.

If you're interested in learning more or becoming involved with The Navigators, go to www.navigators.org. For more discipleship content from The Navigators and NavPress authors, visit www.thedisciplemaker.org. May God bless you in your walk with Him!

Sincerely,

DON PAPE
VP/PUBLISHER, NAVPRESS

www.navpress.com

CP1308